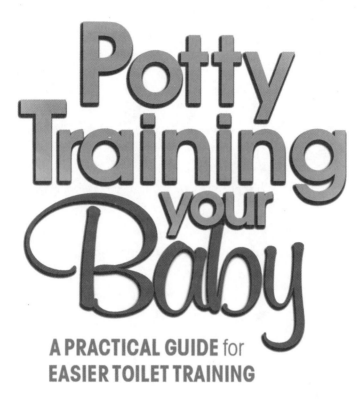

A PRACTICAL GUIDE for
EASIER TOILET TRAINING

KATIE WARREN

SQUAREONE
PUBLISHERS

Cover Design: Jeannie Tudor
Typesetters: Gary A. Rosenberg and
    Theresa Wiscovitch
Illustrations: Vicki Chelf

Square One Publishers
115 Herricks Road
Garden City Park, NY 11040
(516) 535-2010 • (877) 900-BOOK
www.squareonepublishers.com

Library of Congress Cataloging-in-Publication Data

Warren, Katie.
  Potty training your baby : a practical guide for easier toilet training /
Katie Warren.
    p. cm.
  Includes index.
  ISBN 0-7570-0180-7
  1. Toilet training. I. Title.

HQ770.5.W38 2006
649'.62--dc22

                                                            2005020136

Printed in the United States of America

10 9 8 7 6 5 4 3

Contents

To Steve, for making this happen.
To Tiffany, for making it possible.
To Joshua, for reawakening the memories.
To Eli, for the last hurrah.
I love you.

Preface

As a young mother, I never quite understood how potty training could become such a hair-raising experience for parents. Unlike most people I know, all the children in my family were out of diapers before their second birthday. It was something we just did. The women in my family had, for generations, potty trained their babies early. Each generation passing to the next stories that emphasized a light-hearted approach to training. These stories contained a wealth of information. As a result, we just didn't have the problems that seem common in so many families.

After reading everything I could find about the subject and considering the advice offered by many doctors, I began to understand why problems develop. There is a general lack of information on the subject. Most of what parents find to read provides *outmoded* information that is too general and leaves many important questions unanswered. For example, if a two year old refuses to participate, does it mean he's not ready to be trained? Or does it mean you're going about it the wrong way? Could it just be the child's way of expressing his independence? If a one year old pees on the potty whenever he's placed there and seldom wets his diaper, does this mean he's potty trained, or does he have potty-trained parents? Questions such as these create uncertainty for parents. Under the circumstances, even the most rational and intelligent parents can become unglued. It's little wonder that problems develop.

I believe potty training is more of a philosophy than a specific, step-by-step technique. This book presents some new thinking and general guidelines that will help you to potty train your child with minimal stress. With an early start, my method enables you to finish training by the time a lot of parents are just beginning—by the age of one and a half to two years. But regardless of your child's age when you begin, the technique is much the same.

Ultimately, every baby will be potty trained. Every baby *wants* to be potty trained; it's human nature to strive for accomplishment and independence. The baby that is trained early is the one who receives complete support, encouragement, and acceptance from his parents as training progresses. Potty training then becomes a rewarding, bonding experience for both you and you child, which is the way it was meant to be.

1

The Early-Start
Alternative

Potty training is often one of the most frustrating aspects of parenting. For many, it is traumatic. For most, it's never over soon enough. But it doesn't have to be that way. Actually, potty training can be completed a lot sooner than most parents are led to believe. With the right approach, your child can be through with it about the time some say it should begin. It can also be a delightful experience.

The crucial concern for parents has always been *when* to start potty training. In generations past, it was most common for parents to potty train early. Since every diaper soiled meant yet another to hand wash, there was ample incentive. In the 1950s and early 1960s, leading experts advised waiting until a toddler was old enough to comprehend what training was all about and was able to understand its social connotations. They also believed that before any real attempt toward control could be made, the child's sphincter muscles had to be fully developed. At the time, this was thought to occur at approximately twenty-four months of age. Although some still abide by these guidelines, the old point of view is definitely changing. Potty training can begin as early as the child's first year.

We now know that the full development of the sphincter muscles can occur much earlier (between the ages of one and one and a half years), and the argument that a young child lacks the comprehension to be trained has certainly lost credibility. Today, authorities in the field of child development recognize it is really the parents choice whether to begin a child's training early or not. As long as a parent doesn't apply pressure, there now seems to be little expert objection to an early start.

Should you decide to begin training early, you must be realistic.

Potty training isn't accomplished quickly. There are no shortcuts. Early training starts with an emphasis on recognizing sensations and connecting those sensations with the appropriate muscles. Total control isn't possible until the sphincters have fully developed. Potty training is completed once the child himself decides to take full responsibility. With an early start, this may happen at eighteen months, if you have an independent child. Or it may take a little longer, depending on the child's personality.

The typical approach offered to many parents today is based on a child's ability to think about and take care of his own toileting needs almost from the very start of training. Success depends on a child's ability to understand and follow directions. Training begins at approximately age two and can be expected to continue for another six to twelve months. Although most children complete training by the time they are three years old, it is not uncommon to find children up to the age of four who are still wetting their pants.

Many parents find this approach to be frustrating because they recognize their child's readiness to start training as early as the first year. But at that age, they reason a child can't follow instructions. Even at age two years, some children simply won't listen to potty training instructions.

This book provides a system that overcomes these problems. It is designed to meet the emotional needs of your child while teaching control at the same time. Training can begin before the first birthday and can be successfully completed by the second. And it is easily adaptable for older toddlers as well. This system removes the conflict that is so often found in potty training and allows it to become like any other "me-do" project for a child. It's not unlike a child learning to put socks on. Once a process is observed and understood, a young toddler wants to do things for himself. To go to the potty unassisted is simply another avenue for self-expression and independence. No pressure is required to complete potty training. A child does it naturally.

Of course, no child is going to master potty training right away. His sphincter muscles have to mature and he has to learn how to control them. The approach detailed in this book puts your child in touch with muscles that he wouldn't ordinarily notice. Working at it daily, he will soon become aware of the physical sensations related to bowel and bladder control. This is where potty training really begins. With consistent attention, muscle control develops more rapidly. And when the sphincter muscles are finally mature, your child can be in the final stage of potty training—instead of just the beginning. With an early start, your baby could be out of diapers well before the age of two.

CHOICES

Parents today face unique challenges when it comes to potty training. Many intuitively feel they could begin training their babies in the first year, but have virtually no resources to guide them through the process. So, they wait. Others are led to believe that training begun before the second year is simply a waste of time, so they wait. To make the situation all the more confusing, for the first time in history, parents are being influenced by the disposable diaper industry, with advertising that shows big kids using disposables. With the use of super absorbent materials, a child weighing up to forty pounds can easily be accommodated during the training process. Today it is not uncommon for a child to already be playing simple computer games before potty training even begins. Many will be using disposables until age three and older. But it doesn't have to be that way. You absolutely do have a choice. Potty training can be a bonding experience for parents, and an empowering experience for babies. And it can actually be fun!

DOES YOUR CHILD NEED TO KNOW WHAT IT'S ALL ABOUT?

Not really. Control isn't the focus of early training. Awareness is. Recognizing the body's inner workings is always the first step. During the early stages, you will be directing your child's attention towards his body and its functions. Learning to control these functions comes later. Since control isn't an issue during the earliest phase of training, a baby who can sit up by himself is just as able to begin potty training as the toddler. By the time he's reached the second phase of his training, he will have already acquired a good understanding of his bodily functions and spent time exercising some control over them. Regardless of the child's age, the process is much the same.

THE NATURAL RESPONSE

Many parents just don't understand how they could possibly teach their baby something that appears to be so complicated. But it's only complicated if you think it is. Potty training a baby is actually a lot easier than you would imagine.

Babies do most of their communicating on an emotional level. A child "understands" things intuitively a lot sooner than he understands the words and actions attached to those things. So potty training is most successful when you interact with your child in the language he best understands—emotion.

Parents can easily see just how effective "emotional" communication can be. For example, notice what happens when a toddler dances to show off for his parents. Mom and Dad laugh and clap their hands in amusement. And this causes the baby to dance all the more! Not a word has been spoken, yet the child intuitively knows that he is the star attraction and that his audience loves what he is doing. It's the parents' enthusiastic response that gives the child the incentive to keep on dancing. This is the same kind of emotional encouragement that should be applied to potty training.

Obviously, you can't just sit a child down and explain that you want him to start peeing in the potty and expect it to happen. A baby won't understand this. Although he may already know what a wet diaper is, he may not recognize that he has the capability to purposely make it wet. He wets automatically, without any thought or effort.

Potty training involves more than simply teaching a child how to control a physical function. It is actually helping a child to recognize a series of physical sensations, to understand what those sensations mean, and then to control his urge long enough to get to the potty. You can't explain such sensations with words. You must take a different approach and help your child to make the associations in order to discover things *for himself*. The only way you can do this is on an emotional level.

The parents' attitudes and responses provide the key to early potty training. When you place your baby on the potty, your immediate response will tell him exactly what he needs to know. When he starts peeing and you become happy and excited, he not only understands that this is *good*, but that it's also fun! If you do this consistently, within a very short time, he will purposely try to go on the potty just to get that same, happy response from you. This puts him in touch with his body. In the beginning, the joy of sharing his accomplishment is really all that the baby needs. A happy experience provides enough incentive for him to carry on.

Babies Are Geniuses

Let's not underestimate a baby's capabilities. Babies are, by nature, very quick to absorb new experiences. But first, opportunities must be presented. There's really no need to put off potty training until a child is old enough to *tell* you he's tired of wet diapers.

Realize that babies aren't incompetent beings. They simply lack experience. While a baby may not be able to totally control his little system, he can easily grasp the concepts.

CHILDREN THRIVE ON CHALLENGES

Children enjoy learning new skills. They are most attracted to situations that provide a sense of challenge. Learning to walk, drinking from a cup, and feeding themselves all begin as an interesting challenge. The feelings of satisfaction a child experiences each time he makes a little progress are what motivate him to continue his efforts. With each success comes a greater sense of accomplishment and independence.

If a child is given a task to master that lacks some level of challenge to spark his interest, it will be perceived as boring and not worth the trouble.

An example of this problem is the gifted child who fails in school. The problem isn't the inability to learn; the problem is boredom. If the teacher doesn't notice what is happening, the child's lack of interest could easily be misinterpreted. The teacher might begin to expect less of him and he, in turn, will meet those lower expectations and perform far below his potential. The teacher's attitudes and expectations become transferred to the student. Uninspired, his performance level will likely remain below his capabilities.

If the same child were to be placed in an interesting, challenging environment, the opportunity to stimulate his mind is enhanced. He might easily become the star pupil in the class.

The same principle can be applied to potty training. Recognize what your child is capable of. Create a challenge that is attainable. Make it interesting and you'll create a training experience that encourages participation.

MUSCLE MATURITY

The sphincter muscles control the bowels and bladder. Some doctors tell us they mature between twenty and twenty-four months of age. So they say it's useless to try to potty train any earlier. But this time frame is only an estimate. It is misleading because it represents the *oldest age* at which a child's sphincter muscles are expected to develop, not the average age. It also implies that a child lacks any and all control over his system until complete development has occurred. This is absolutely false.

The average baby's nervous system has matured enough to allow complete voluntary control of the sphincter muscles by the time he's reached eighteen months of age. Some babies complete this process as early as twelve months. For others, complete development may not occur before twenty-four months of age.

Since children's bodies develop at their own individual paces, this book's system is designed to work with the immature sphincter muscles as their natural maturing process continues. This training system encourages the development of the sphincter muscles to a degree, but it is nature that completes the cycle. The only way you'll really know when the process is complete is when the training is over. At best, your observations will tell you that your child is making progress and gaining more control as time goes on.

POTTY TRAINING TAKES TIME

It is important to remember that potty training cannot be completed until the sphincter muscles are fully mature, regardless of your child's age or the amount of training. However, it can be started much earlier because even immature sphincter muscles send out sensations. Because early training concerns itself entirely with recognizing these sensations, the lack of complete muscular development is unimportant.

Every physical thing a child does requires practice. Babies don't start walking around the house as soon as they learn to stand. Their muscles aren't developed enough and they lack having full control of them. They take a few steps, then fall flat on their fannies. They hold on to Mom or Dad's fingers and slowly waddle across the room. With such little day-by-day efforts, they get better and better and their muscles become stronger and stronger. Soon, little feet are pattering all around the house. The same thing happens with potty training. Practice encourages the development of control as the sphincter muscles mature.

All babies go through the same stages and experiences while being trained. This process takes months, *regardless of the child's age.* A baby must learn what it feels like to be wet, to associate wetting with the muscles involved, to recognize the feelings of a bowel movement or the need to go to the potty. As the baby becomes aware of the muscles involved, he naturally begins to use them. The more often he does this, the more familiar he becomes with the muscles. The more familiar he is with the muscles, the more he will try to use them and the stronger those muscles become. As the muscles become stronger, he learns to control himself for longer and longer periods of time.

Once your baby is fully aware of all the sensations, he'll go on to the final stages of potty training. He'll learn to communicate his needs to you and, finally, to use his potty on his own. This last step is the *only* one that cannot occur until the sphincter muscles have completed their growth process. So instead of waiting until muscle development is complete before beginning, your child will already be in the final stages of training.

ENCOURAGING SELF MOTIVATION

One of the most fundamental aspects of potty training is consistently overlooked. That is the emotional gratification that motivates a child to try new experiences. Learning is as natural for a child as breathing. Learning comes easier if we provide an atmosphere of encouragement without making excessive demands. It's believed that we should provide enough stimulation and excitement for the child's mind to thrive, yet not so much that he becomes overwhelmed. We must achieve a balance. If we push too hard or expect more than he can deliver, he will withdraw, become frustrated, or angry.

You can't *force* a child to acquire a new skill. He learns because he is motivated to do so. He does this naturally, in a very spontaneous way.

A child motivates himself in many ways and, without interference, his inner drive serves as the catalyst for growth. Toddlers can be prompted to try just about anything if they are led to believe the activity is fun or interesting. They never sit and reason out a situation before trying it. They do not consider their limitations. They are drawn to experience life and everything it has to offer. We see examples of this constantly as we watch our children grow.

For example, a one year old may decide to start brushing his teeth because he sees his parents doing so. He wants to be like his parents; to be included in their rituals. He brushes his teeth to be like them, not because he wants to avoid cavities. His knowledge is much too limited to consider such things, but he is motivated to try. By trying, he learns.

If his efforts are encouraged, the personal gratification he experiences will prompt him to try again. So tooth brushing will become a habit long before he learns the real reason why he's doing it.

PARENTS KNOW BEST

Ordinarily, parents are encouraged to stimulate their child's development in every area—physical and mental. But potty training seems to be the only area of development that is treated differently.

Many in the field of child development still regard potty training as an entirely physical process that the child must learn to control with logical decision-making. They believe that potty training shouldn't be started until around the second birthday, since the baby's mind must be mature enough to "think" about it first.

Pediatricians can be just as narrow-minded. Most really don't give potty training much thought. It isn't uncommon for them to lack any firm opinions about it and to quickly pass over the subject with "off-the-cuff' advice. Many base their opinions on the belief that a child must be old enough to be "taught" with words and firm direction. This approach to training provides little incentive for the child. Since the toddler's emotional needs and development are totally overlooked, such a training experience becomes quite limited.

Unfortunately, many parents are willing to accept the myth that children under two are just too young to comprehend potty training. They'll ignore their own intuition and wait longer than necessary to begin potty training because some experts say it can't be done. As a result, we now have toddlers who are able to count and recite their ABCs, yet are still in diapers. It's one thing to delay training because you just don't care to get started. It's quite another to wait because you've received inadequate advice, leading you to believe that you don't have a choice in the matter. Because you do!

Children are emotional beings, driven by curiosity to participate in and observe every little thing. They are filled with emotion. Every aspect of their well-being is communicated on an emotional level first. Every interest is shared. You communicate with them emotionally, too. You send them messages by your smiles, your tone of voice and your touch. Your attitude is a powerful influence that can support learning and self-discovery. And by taking a positive, realistic approach, you can help them to learn anything you want them to learn—like using the potty.

BETTER TO START SOONER THAN LATER

I believe it is best to begin training at a time in a baby's development that compliments and encourages the early stages of training. This usually occurs well before the child's second year. For many children, it's even before the first birthday.

Nothing should be asked of a child that is not within his reach. On the other hand, don't handicap your child by underestimating his ability.

It's a mistake to assume that a child must be at least two years old to begin training. By his second year, a toddler is entering a period of development that makes training more difficult. The two year old is driven by a budding sense of independence that at times overwhelms both him and his parents. He's argumentative and contrary. He doesn't want to be reminded that there are things that he still doesn't know. He much prefers to believe that he knows all he needs to know. The growing awareness that he is a separate being with a mind of his own must be constantly tested. Two year olds want to assert themselves. To the toddler, potty training is just another situation that must be "handled." His instinct is to dig in his heels and holler, just to make a point.

By the time is has reached age two, he has missed the most ideal time to begin or to accept the idea of potty training. To expect a rambunctious two year old to stop what he's doing to sit on the potty is going against his grain. At age two, the pleasant, submissive stage is over.

This isn't to imply that training a toddler is impossible—only that certain problems are more likely to develop. His behavior is shifting from dependency to that of independence. Since he can't be expected to handle his needs on his own, he must constantly ask for help. This is something a two year old often finds difficult to do. After all, being in control is most important to him at this time. Asking for assistance, would mean giving up that control.

This situation can be avoided when you begin a child's training when he's younger. Then you're dealing with an entirely different situation. A baby's developmental stage compliments the early steps of potty training. In the first year, the average child has become particularly interested in other people and their responses to his behavior. He tries to imitate behavior and takes pride in his achievements. He loves the company of his parents and their involvement in his activities.

By twelve months, he's fully aware of his audience. He likes to repeat performances that generate excitement and laughter. He enjoys the social give-and-take. He's learned to anticipate attention, excitement, and praise when he does something new or special. His parents are the major influence in his life, which suits him just fine. He's cooperative because it is the only way he knows how to be.

These are the attributes that allow potty training to go most smoothly because you are asking your child to do something that is natural for him at this stage of development. He is thrilled to participate, and learning about his body delights him. His frame of mind encourages curiosity and participation in the training. When you potty train your child in a gentle, relaxed manner, he is blessed with the best possible experience. Progress comes gradually. As it does, his self-confidence and sense of identity are enhanced.

By the time he enters a more independent stage, your child will be in a position to put what he's learned about himself into action. He will complete his own training by his own initiative, not yours. The focal point of training is not to obtain quick control. The main point is to encourage the child to *want* to take control of his body, which he does in an easy and relaxed way.

2

Basic Elements Needed

There's a process, a method to potty training that can be broken down into three segments. Training begins by first helping a child to recognize a series of physical sensations and to understand what they mean. The second step is helping him to connect those sensations with the appropriate muscles and practice with them. Finally, in the third step, he learns purposeful control of his functions until complete control is achieved.

The first two steps involve a child's experiencing and recognizing the body's functions. This is where the bulk of your child's training takes place. It doesn't happen overnight. Progress comes in small steps. Regardless of his age, a child cannot move into the final stage of training until he has a full understanding of his body. And while the first two steps of training take the most time, a child does not have to intellectually understand the process in order to learn from the experience.

There are four elements necessary in order for training to begin. These are: a healthy baby, a baby who is capable of sitting up by himself, a relaxed attitude, and a sturdy potty.

A HEALTHY BABY

Do not try to potty train a sick baby. If your child is having health problems, it is best for everyone involved that you delay potty training. When a person feels bad physically, it's very easy to become upset. If a toddler becomes irritated at having to deal with the potty when he does not feel well, he may develop a negative mindset. This is the very thing that you want to avoid. New learning experiences require confidence, desire, and energy. Illness depletes these natural attributes. If your child is ill, put the potty away until another day. If your child has experienced serious health problems, don't begin training until the entire convalescent period is over.

A BABY WHO CAN SIT UP BY HIMSELF

You can't begin training until your baby is able to sit up all by himself. He should be able to sit for at least thirty minutes without having to rely on the extra support of his hands or props. If your child sits in a slumped position, leaning sideways or forward, then he's not yet ready for potty training.

The ability to sit is determined mostly by the back and abdominal muscles. In a baby's development, this can occur as early as five months. But some babies don't sit up until the ninth month or later. Under no circumstances should you consider beginning potty training before this time. These muscles must be sufficiently developed to easily support and steady his upper trunk as he sits on the potty. Starting training before the baby can sit confidently by himself could magnify his natural fear of falling and losing control. So let your baby master sitting before you begin putting him on the potty.

A RELAXED ATTITUDE

The attitude we take toward anything we do directly affects the success of our effort. *A relaxed and positive attitude on your part is the most important element in successful potty training.*

A child learns best in an atmosphere that is free of anxiety. Surely the world is an imperfect place, and nobody lives in an entirely stress-free environment. There is stress even in the most perfect of homes. But potty training is an area of development that needs special attention. We must be careful to avoid unnecessary stress. Keep cool, no matter what happens.

Don't pay much attention to the potty training advice of other people. Unwise or outmoded theories can often create real stress for parents. Everyone has an opinion about potty training that they can't wait to pass on to you. But few people are really aware of the facts. So try to maintain your emotional balance and ignore any negative ideas that may hinder your progress.

A child learns best in an atmosphere that is free of anxiety.

It's Not a Contest

Stress and anxiety can also be created when parents feel that their child's accomplishments (or lack of them) are a reflection of their parenting abilities. This thinking is not only wrong, it creates conflict between parent and child.

Don't let potty training become some kind of contest. We live in a highly competitive society in which contests and games play an important role in our social development. Certainly, our children's physical accomplishments are sources of great pride. Parents love to brag about how "quickly" their baby does something and how smart he is. And that's okay. But when taken a step too far, pride may actually become a catalyst for anxiety. Don't allow potty training to become your child's first "failure."

Yes, early potty training is certainly something to be proud of. But it's not a contest. That's not the point at all. A child doesn't "win" by finishing earlier than anyone else. If you allow yourself to become a judge, a referee, or a "scorekeeper," you'll do more harm than good.

Potty Training Helps Shape a Child's Self-Image

Understand that potty training means more to a child than just mastering his toilet needs. Potty training is a child's first, true self-image experience. All aspects of training influence the child's awareness of himself and provide a sense of his place in the world. How he perceives his body and himself when he's older is often dictated by the experiences he has during this training. The ramifications are broad, complex, and life-long.

We all have our own emotional baggage, the roots of which began at infancy. Since training usually covers a period of six months to one year, many impressions can be implanted in your child's mind. Try to make them positive ones. Remember that the elimination of wastes is an entirely normal and healthy process. Babies don't have negative feelings about these functions unless *you* create them. Learning to sit on the potty should be a pleasure, not an ordeal, and certainly not a judgment of success or failure. If the experience is a positive one, your child will be free to develop a more confident attitude towards himself. This positive self-image will follow him into adulthood.

Of course, every child perceives these experiences in his own way, and you can only do so much to enhance your child's self-image. However, you can avoid creating harmful, unnecessary problems. If you maintain a positive attitude about everything connected with potty training, you can help him to become a more emotionally well-balanced person.

A STURDY POTTY

The selection of a potty is very important. Many different styles are available, and a wrong choice could present problems. For example, some models are unsteady and can easily tip over. Others are designed for a small child and allow no room for growth. Most models have detachable splatter cups, but some don't allow the cup to be locked into place. So the child may constantly pull the cup up and out and urinate over the rim—and onto the floor!

Take your child with you when you go to buy a potty. Sit him on different models and make sure the fit is right. There should be plenty of room on the sides and behind the baby's bottom to accommodate future growth. Remember—babies grow quickly, and that should be taken into consideration as you make your final choice.

Most of today's models are constructed entirely of plastic. The most unsteady ones have straight sides and/or a narrow base. When the child leans just a bit too far to the left or right, the whole thing can easily flip onto its side. Narrow-based potties are an open invitation to disaster. If you decide on a "commode" model buy one that's constructed with a wider rim of plastic around the base (which flares out to give more stability).

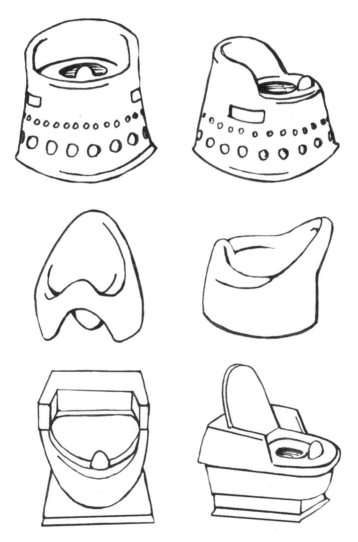

Examples of flare-bottomed potties (front and side views).

Some models are built to resemble a little chair with a hole in the seat. Unless it is made with extra supports across the base, it will not be steady enough for a toddler to use safely. Regardless of the style you're considering, sit your child on the potty. Lean his body in all directions to see if the base has any tendency to lift off the floor.

Potties with Armrests Are Not Recommended

Avoid armrests. When a child leans to one side, they tend to hold the armrest (which exerts extra leverage). This makes the chair exceptionally easy to tip over. In addition, the armrests make the act of sitting down on the potty more precarious. Babies simply don't sit down on these things without using their hands. They grab the armrest as they are backing onto the chair to sit. Unless they grab both armrests and back straight onto the chair (something few babies are capable of doing), they can flip the chair onto its side even before their fanny hits the seat. A baby only has to have this happen once before deciding that the thing is more trouble than it's worth. If you want a chair-like model, find one that has a broad base with very sturdy legs. Also keep in mind that the heavier it is, the better.

The Best Potties Stay Firmly in Place

The best potties are more rounded and shaped like an inverted, rounded cone. The base is circular and much wider than the upper half, where the child sits. No matter how far a child leans, the potty stays firmly in place on the floor.

Some potties offer a built-in music box. This is supposed to keep the baby interested and entertained as he sits on it. That's okay, I suppose. But the problem is that the music box is usually positioned behind the child's back. So the first thing the child does when the music starts to play is to twist out of his sitting position to investigate the box. Little people love gadgets, but having one on a potty diverts a baby's attention away from the potty training to the potty itself.

Examine a Potty Thoroughly Before Purchase

You'll also find models designed with a removable seat section that may be placed on an adult toilet. The instructions for some give the impression that all you have to do is snap the potty top on and off whenever you want. This is a great idea, if it works as it's supposed to. I bought one of these, thinking how simple it would be! Only I found the lid nearly impossible to remove from the potty. We eventually had to use tools to take off what had been advertised as an "easy-to-remove" seat. It turned out to be just as difficult to put back on as it was to get off. So be sure to check everything over carefully before you buy.

When selecting a potty, always examine the splatter cup. Girls as well as boys will need this piece attached to the potty. When the cup is in place, make sure it fits comfortably between your child's legs. The cup itself should not press into the baby's groin area. If you can place a finger between the cup and the baby without touching either one, then the fit is right. If you can't, then the fit is too snug.

When Buying a Potty

Features to Look For

- ❑ Stability!
- ❑ Plenty of space on the sides and behind the baby's bottom.
- ❑ Wider rim around the base, or added support for stability.
- ❑ Shaped like an inverted, rounded cone.
- ❑ A base that is wider than the area your baby sits upon.
- ❑ A splatter cup that fits comfortably between the baby's legs, for both boys and girls.
- ❑ Ample space between the splatter cup and the baby's body.

Features to Avoid

- Any potty that tips if your child leans in any direction.
- Straight sides and/or a narrow base.
- Armrests.
- Built-in music box at the back.
- Seat straps.

Seat Straps Are Not Good Features

You will find seat straps available on many models. They give the impression that the baby is safer, but that's actually a misconception. Any potty can be tipped over by an active baby who wants to get *up*. If the straps are fastened when the baby stands, the potty will go with him. Besides, a baby perceives being tied down as a form of punishment. You certainly don't want him to have that kind of feeling about his potty! Finally, remember never to turn your back on a small baby who is sitting on the potty. Accidents happen in the blink of an eye, so be careful.

Potties versus Toilets

Why buy a potty? Won't the toilet do? Unless you are training an older toddler, the answer to this question is *no*. Trying to use a full-size toilet

Example of a child using a step-up.

at the beginning of training creates too many problems. The reasons are understandable. The most obvious is that the toilet was designed to accommodate an adult's body. From a tot's point of view, a toilet's size can be very intimidating.

If you want your child to be able to use both the potty *and* the toilet, I would advise purchasing a separate potty top in addition to the potty. These are inexpensive and can be found wherever potty chairs are sold. But don't substitute a potty chair top that can be placed on an adult toilet for a real potty. They're okay for travel use and in the later stages of your child's training, but aren't a suitable replacement for his own potty.

Your child needs a potty he'll be able to master all by himself. He should have a potty that he's able to sit on comfortably and with ease. This helps him to develop confidence and encourages him to proceed to the final stages of training.

For a small child, the idea of using a regular toilet without assistance is unrealistic. An adult toilet can deny him the feeling of self-competence. And without confidence, potty training is far more difficult to achieve. Such frustration is counter-productive to the training process.

After your child has made good progress on his own little potty, then he can begin using the adult toilet, perhaps with the aid of a step-up or stool. By this time, his sense of balance will be perfected. The toilet routine will be "old hat," so you won't have to worry about it (and neither will your child).

TIME TO GET STARTED

As presented in this chapter, once you have the necessary elements for potty training—a healthy baby who can sit up by himself, a relaxed and positive attitude on your part, and a safe, sturdy potty—you can help your child begin this normal, healthy process. Feel confident that with your gentle yet focused guidance, he will find success in this, his first true self-image experience.

3

The One Year Old

abies are a lot smarter and more capable than most people imagine. They are also highly impressionable. The way you approach a child during potty training affects the way he'll begin to feel about himself deep within. So to have the best possible training experience, to make it progress easily, you must create an atmosphere where babies have fun as they learn and gain competence, where pride and achievement can be displayed daily.

Potty training should offer a baby the added enjoyment of dazzling his parents by his very existence. The training should encourage a child to express himself fully, without fear of criticism. Negative reinforcements (like scolding and guilt trips) should never enter into the training process. Bit by bit, these parental negatives chip away a child's confidence and sense of self-worth. In such case, training takes longer to complete and is usually beset by problems.

With a stress-free method of potty training, you avoid the problems usually associated with early training. This system provides the guidelines necessary to boost the sense of pride and accomplishment that is so necessary for a child's emotional well-being. In many ways, it may be said that this system gives your child the opportunity to potty train himself—and to do so at a very early age.

A BIG EXPERIENCE

Potty training is a big experience for babies and toddlers. It's much more than a physical activity. It contributes to their emotional development as well. With proper guidance, potty training will provide the

21

building blocks for your child's self-esteem and encourage a better self-image. So *how* you interact with your child is of fundamental importance. If you demand more from your child than he can deliver, you are setting the stage for disappointment. This erodes self-confidence and slows down the training. With positive experiences, a child learns that he is *important* and that he can *control his environment.*

A child's behavior mirrors his self-image. When he feels good about himself, he becomes more involved, more outgoing, and less threatened. He learns to trust himself and others. A positive and enlightened atmosphere will always bring out the best in your child and will enhance the entire potty training experience.

Your Goal

Your goal is to guide your child in such a way that he can discover how his body works. During the process, he'll gain valuable experience as he experiments with his body. By the time he reaches the point where his sphincter muscles are completely developed, he will be fully capable of finishing his training.

As training progresses, always consider what developmental phase your child is in. Since babies and toddlers pass through different stages at different times, it is up to you to recognize your child's emotional and physical needs and to stay in tune with him. He's maturing and changing almost daily. Adjust yourself to your child as he grows. The training experience should never be allowed to become mundane or boring.

Once a child has become accustomed to the fundamental aspects of training, introduce him to some responsibilities. Allow him to actively participate in the decision-making. For example, ask him if he'd like to drop the wet diaper in the diaper pail. At first, you'll have to answer "yes" for him, but he'll soon get the idea. Ask him if he will carry the diaper for you as you take it to the pail. Let him drop it in. As soon as a child begins to walk, allow him to dispose of his wet diaper by himself. If he doesn't want to carry it to the pail, ask him if he wants you to do it for him. This keeps him involved and stimulates his sense of power and accomplishment.

Whenever possible, let him fetch a new diaper for you when he needs a change. When you begin to help him onto the toilet, if you have more than one in your home, allow him to choose which one he will use next. Allow him to flush the toilet with every opportunity that comes his way. When he gets into training pants, buy them in different colors and let him decide which color he wants to wear.

Girls and Boys

Little girls should be encouraged to wipe after urinating as soon as they begin to walk. They love this kind of participation. Since tots like to imitate, don't be concerned if your son wants to wipe after peeing, as well. Let him. It's no big deal. But, I do suggest that you introduce your son to the practice of getting that last drop of urine off. A man will do this with a little shake, but a tap or two is a more appropriate action for a tot to accomplish.

Your Encouragement

Don't limit yourself to the suggestions provided in this book. Use your imagination while training your child. Encourage his involvement. It really isn't easy being a little kid. Everyone seems to be constantly bossing them around. As a child approaches fifteen or sixteen months old, he becomes very aware of this and recognizes his vulnerabilities. This, in itself, is enough to cause a child to become rebellious. By allowing him to make choices, you will help to alleviate some of his tension. And you will benefit from this just as much as he does. Training will run more smoothly and end earlier simply because your child participates and is taught to assume control. Your encouragement lifts your child's self-esteem. Most importantly, it lets your child know that you have faith in his ability, that you trust and respect him.

When Baby Balks

If you have a young one who absolutely hates to have a diaper change, you're probably wondering how on earth you are ever going to get that baby interested in sitting on the potty. My feeling is that you're probably not; at least not until your little one gets a bit more settled. There are many reasons why a baby will get upset at the idea of a diaper change. Usually, it's just a matter of excess stimulation. It's a busy time physically and emotionally. To your baby, learning to talk and walk is extremely exciting, like any situation or change in routine that takes him into a new environment. Whatever the cause, babies don't ordinarily balk for long. So why fight? Wait for a while. As soon as diapering becomes less of a struggle, you might consider introducing the potty then. Whatever you do, don't make this a contentious issue.

An Educational Experience

Potty training is an educational experience. To approach it in any other way would be wrong. It doesn't matter how old the child is—learning takes time. Children progress at their own pace in potty training, as with all physical tasks. All you can do is provide the proper setting with your support, your encouragement, and, most of all, your respect. The rest is up to him. The following guidelines are simple to follow. This technique eliminates trauma, anger, and pain for both the parent and child. Whether you're beginning your child's training at nine months or at two years, the bottom line is that *potty training should be a time of bonding, learning, and enjoyment.*

When to Begin

Potty training can actually start as soon as a baby is able to sit up on his own and remain sitting for a good while without support. This is actually the most natural time for the baby to begin. At this age, babies are quite limited in their ability to get around. They're also limited in the amount of things they can do. They depend on you to take them from one place to another, to give them their favorite toy, to entertain them. You are the gateway to all their new experiences. The new things that you show them are received with open joy and curiosity. For the baby who has just recently mastered sitting on his own, getting to sit up on a potty is terrific fun. Babies are usually very eager to "show their stuff' and are filled with pride as they do so. With a happy and relaxed attitude on your part, you set the foundation for effective potty training.

Put the Potty Where Your Baby Spends Time

When you first bring the potty home, put it in the room where your baby spends the most time. He'll be more comfortable and at ease there. It doesn't have to be in the bathroom. In fact, the bathroom might be counter-productive in the early stages of potty training. Bathrooms are places of amazement for a baby, filled with exciting colors, smells, and objects that can easily divert his attention from you and the job at hand. You want him to focus on his bodily sensations and his potty, not on the shower curtain, towels, or soap dish.

There will be plenty of time to move the potty into the bathroom. For now, a familiar place will work more to your advantage. If that happens to be the den, kitchen or the living room, don't worry about comments from visitors. When you explain why it's there, guests will understand and probably be amused. If not, it's their problem not yours.

THE TRAINING EXPERIENCE

Babies commonly wet themselves approximately twenty minutes after having their milk. Like most adults, they also urinate immediately after waking from sleep.

For the first three or four weeks, try to catch your baby just before the act. Place him on the potty immediately after he wakes from a nap and twenty minutes or so after he drinks his milk. Sit him there for only two or three minutes. As you wait, hold his attention by talking to him and giving him a small object to play with (however, no food while on the potty, please).

Make it a quiet time of gentle communication between the two of you. If he pees in the potty, show your excitement. Point out to him that he is wetting *while he is doing so*. He'll react to your response and will soon realize just what it is he's doing that is causing all your excitement!

My daughter, who is now grown-up, was completely potty trained at eighteen months. Although I certainly helped her with wiping, I no longer had to take her to her potty. She went on her own. I started Tiffany's training early by placing her on her new potty twenty minutes after she finished nursing. Much to my delight, the first time I put her on the potty, she started to pee. I started hopping around, acting like a clown, laughing and pointing into the potty and saying "pee-pee." I'm sure I might have looked ridiculous, but she loved the show. I let her look at the pee in the potty, then we took it into the bathroom and flushed it. And though she may not have understood all I was saying, I told her exactly what we were doing each step of the way. We repeated this scenario three times each day.

Of course, she didn't always wet, but when she did, I went into my clowning routine. By the end of the first week, whenever I put Tiff on the potty, she would concentrate so hard her little face would turn red as she strained to pee. The second she started, she'd look my way and give the biggest grin. She wanted me to clown and dance around the room, which I promptly did. It was great fun. My playful approach made peeing in the potty a game. The game encouraged her own playfulness and creat-ed a very receptive attitude. This also gave her total control over the sit-uation, which presented her with an opportunity she simply could not resist. There were no expectations and no pressure—there was only fun.

That was our beginning. Within that first week, she discovered the muscles which make bladder control possible and started focusing her attention on them.

Always remember that a pleasant attitude must be maintained. Potty training should be fun. Babies love to learn. They love little games and they love to do things that get positive reactions from Mom and Dad. If your child sees that you're having a good time, he's more likely to get into the spirit of it all. Your good, playful attitude is transferred to the baby. As a result, the learning process is speeded up, and your baby gets trained much sooner.

Wet and Dry

During these first few weeks, it's very important to go slowly. Keep dia-pers dry. Check often and change your baby's diaper as soon as he wets or poops. The primary reason for this is so your child can make simple comparisons between the feel of wet and dry. If you are using dispos-ables, this would be an ideal time to get the ones that have a lesser absorbency to use, at least during the day. Higher absorbency diapers are meant to draw moisture away from baby's skin and keep baby dry. They remove the opportunity for the baby to connect urination with the sensation of wetness.

When changing your baby, talk to him. Tell him you're changing his diaper because this one is wet or poopy. Tell him this as a point of infor-mation, never with even a hint of disapproval. Also, whenever he pass-es gas, bring that to his attention. This will focus his attention on yet another of his body's functions.

As you do all this, you're acquainting your child with his body. In essence, you're helping to develop his whole attitude toward the potty and toilet training. You want it to be a totally positive experience. Make it a fun, sharing experience.

A Supportive Attitude

Potty training should never become a war of wills. *Don't pressure your child for results.* If you do, he'll develop an attitude problem. Imagine how you'd feel if someone dictated when and where you'd go next, hovering over you all the while, waiting. Babies are people, too! Always treat your child with respect. Keep in mind that you're dealing with his self-esteem here. If your child doesn't have to pee, then accept that. Take him off the potty and tell him he didn't need to pee as you put his diaper back on. Furthermore, make sure he knows that *it's okay when he doesn't!* The more supportive your attitude, the more enjoyable the whole experience will be for your baby.

Always take into consideration how the day is progressing for your child. If he's overly tired, fussy from lack of sleep, or bothered by teething, then skip sitting him on the potty. If family or guests are visiting and the normal routine has been disrupted, then wait until the next day to resume training.

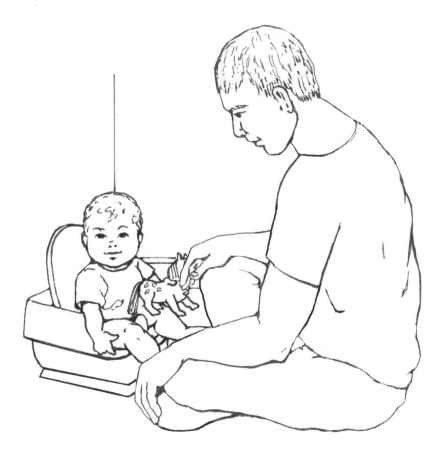

Potty training should be a pleasant, postive experience.

Talking to Your Baby

Talk to your child whenever you're helping him with his toilet needs. Ask him if he has to pee before taking him to the potty. Tell him you're taking his diaper off so he can pee on the potty. Tell him you're changing his diaper because he's wet or has pooped. As he urinates on the potty, tell him what's happening as it is happening. If he sits on the potty and nothing happens, tell him so. Express your pleasure when he does go, but remember to tell him it's okay when he doesn't. Be his friend. Tell him all about it. He might not understand everything you're saying at first, but he will soon enough.

Once your child understands the meaning of your words, he may sometimes get a little ahead of himself. Many a parent can relate the story of approaching their dry baby, telling him it's time to pee, then finding a warm wet diaper upon arriving at the potty. This isn't a real problem, just a miscue. Your child did exactly what was asked of him— he just did it too soon! If this happens to you regularly, don't mention the key words "pee" or "potty" until the diaper is off. Words become signals, and misunderstandings come easy for small children. If you change your phrasing, the problem should disappear in no time.

Stepping Up Training

A baby progresses at his own individual pace. Remember that your child will not necessarily need to urinate simply because you are placing him on his potty. Watch him carefully and be encouraging, but don't try to push ahead too quickly. As he becomes acquainted with his potty and begins to use it fairly regularly, you can begin to step things up a bit.

Start putting your baby on the potty at _twenty-minute intervals during the day_. Ask him if he needs to pee. Then tell him what you are doing to help him each time. The phrases you use will quickly be remembered and understood. And you will soon be pleasantly surprised to find him indicating either a "yes" or a "no" in his own little way when you ask him if he needs to pee.

Initially, you need to follow this twenty-minute schedule for only two or three hours a day. As you work with your child, you'll learn his habits and be able to catch him with amazing accuracy. This will enable him to more fully associate the process of removing the diaper, then sitting on the potty to urinate. Be observant. Watch for clues that indicate it's time to go to the potty. Once you learn his schedule, you can adjust the twenty-minute interval to suit him. Some babies have an innate ability to hold their urine for quite some time. As soon as you're aware of his pattern, approach your baby approximately five to ten minutes before he would ordinarily wet.

If he doesn't urinate, simply tell him so as you take him off the potty. Then try again ten or fifteen minutes later. After all, you aren't making a demand for performance from your child—you're giving him an opportunity. Always show your approval with each accomplishment. *Never put pressure on your baby. Never show disappointment.*

Disrupted Sleeping Patterns

As potty training progresses, your child may experience some problems sleeping at night. His bladder is small, and as he gains more control of it, he'll often wake up instead of wetting in his sleep. Some babies do this more than others. At this point in the training, many babies start to wet, then hold in the rest and cry out for help. These are indications that the child is beginning to gain more voluntary control of his sphincter muscles, even though they have not yet completed their development. If he does wake up at night and his diaper is dry or only a little wet, place him on his potty without delay. He'll probably be quite fussy since he's not fully awake, so be especially gentle and reassuring.

If he doesn't urinate quickly after you sit him on the potty, put the diaper back on and lull him back to sleep. This restlessness shouldn't last long, so be patient. Soon, he'll remain dry until morning—just like you.

Learning by Watching

As you're potty training your baby, remember you are also introducing him to one of the most fascinating things in your house: the toilet. Let your child go with you into the bathroom when you dump his potty into the toilet. Let him flush it. Let him see that you use the big potty. Let him flush the toilet after you use it. Tell him all about it! Toilets are great fun. But be aware that they can also be dangerous. Babies love to splash their hands in the toilet water. They also enjoy seeing their own reflections in it. Don't be mad, but do teach your baby that *big toilets are not for play.* They have only one purpose. *Make a habit of closing all toilet lids after each use.* There have been cases where babies have actually

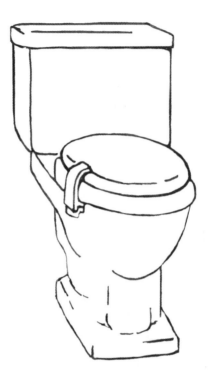

**A toilet seat lock will prevent your child
from playing with toilet water.**

fallen into the toilet headfirst and drowned. This is one mistake no one should have to suffer the consequences of.

Your baby will probably develop a fascination with his own potty, especially if it has a lid. This is normal and is part of the learning experience. Keep the potty very clean and let the child play with it as much as he likes. *But be aware that little fingers can sometimes get pinched by the lid.* If this happens often, lay the potty on its side until he's better able to manage.

When Baby Starts to Take Over

Within a few months, your baby will have it all figured out. He won't have complete control of his sphincters, but he will know when it's about time to go. He may want to tell you it's potty time, but be unable to communicate it clearly. This can be frustrating for a baby and can make him suddenly cranky. It's only natural for people to get upset when they've "got to go" and can't get to the bathroom. So when your baby starts fussing, it could be his way of saying "potty time."

By this time, your child should clearly understand you when you talk about the potty. So when he turns fussy, ask him if he's got to go. He may indicate that's exactly what he wants. If so, get him there quickly.

Sometimes you'll get mixed signals. A baby may be fussing because his bladder is full, but won't want to take the time to have his diaper taken off, then have it put back on again. He knows this routine and it can get a little boring. To him, it seems like a long time to wait around before getting back to play. So when he's fussing and you ask if he needs to pee and he gets even fussier, he may not mean "no." He may really mean "yes, I've got to go but I'm not pleased about it 'cause I was having fun and now I've got to stop while you work with my diaper!" You'll have to use your intuition to figure out when "no" really means "yes."

Help your baby onto his potty immediately as soon as he exhibits a need during the day. Always show your child that you're there for him. This encourages him to communicate with you all the more. Monitor his schedule because it will lengthen quickly as he grows. Take potty breaks as soon as you think you've gotten one of his cues.

However, if he begins to protest on the way to the potty, respect his wishes. You don't want the act of sitting on the potty to feel like a form of punishment. Even if he ends up wetting or messing his diapers a few minutes later, don't let it upset you. You are still making progress. He did hold it in for a while, after all. Those muscles are getting stronger. He's learning.

Emptying the Potty

Now let's talk about how you should empty the potty. For the younger baby, just empty it into a regular toilet, saying "Let's put _____ [whatever it is he did] in the big potty." Most kids love to watch the toilet water flush, so take your child with you as you empty and flush. When they see that they're participating by contributing whatever it is that's being flushed, they become even more fascinated. However, once this enthusiasm grabs hold of your baby, he'll start trying to put anything and everything into the toilet. So keep a close eye on him.

Some children are frightened by the sound of the toilet flushing.

They might even begin to associate this fear with bladder and bowel movements. I've never seen such a child myself, but if it happens to your child, then don't dispose of the waste in his presence. Give him time, and then begin to occasionally flush the unused toilet. The problem will soon resolve itself.

Most babies take a special delight in flushing the toilet. As soon as your child is able to reach the handle and has the strength to make it flush, let him do it whenever he's in the bathroom. You might also let him turn off the light as you exit the bathroom. This gives him more to experience, a sense of power and accomplishment. Again, encourage your child to keep you company in the bathroom. Be happy, and let him see that all is well. As your toddler gains experience, he'll probably want to empty his potty himself. Rather than discourage him, let him take his potty to the toilet. Don't turn it into a negative, "you can't" situation. Stay close to avoid any spills, but if you can, let him try to do it himself.

Training Pants

Once you have the confidence that your baby has progressed sufficiently, you'll begin to move from diapers to training pants. Moving into training pants marks the time when a child shifts into a new mode of thinking and responsibility towards staying dry. It also represents to a child the shift in attitude of the parent toward them. This is very significant for toddlers. They know they've progressed and the training panty is very symbolic of this change.

Some parents may wonder why use the cotton panty as opposed to a pull-up disposable. In every way, the cotton training panty feels different. They are soft and smooth fitting. And, if your child accidentally begins to wet in them, the warmth of urine soaking into the panty causes an *immediate response*. Unlike any pull-up on the market, when you wet the cotton panty, urine will continue down the leg and onto the floor. Some toddlers get upset at first because it comes as quite a surprise to suddenly find themselves standing in a puddle of urine. This really gets their attention. It will happen, so be prepared.

The differences between a disposable pull-up and a cotton training panty is significant. Although many pull-ups allow a child to feel some wetness, they still prevent leaking just like ordinary disposables do. There is no real incentive for a child to try to stop the flow. This is why I recommend cotton training pants.

There are several types of panties your child can wear. Styles that offer three-, four-, or five-ply protection are best. Single-layer terry-cloth panties shouldn't be used until your child has reduced his number of accidents to a minimum, since they provide the least absorbency.

Make sure the panties you buy are big enough for your child to easily pull down by himself. You don't want your child to become frustrated because his panties are stuck! If they are too snug over the hips, they'll bunch up as your child tries to pull them down. Pay particular attention to the leg openings. There should be enough elastic for ample stretch. If possible, try a pair on your child to be sure.

Since an "accident" in training pants will also wet the floor, it's best for your child to start wearing them for short periods when you are nearby. If you're going to be too busy to quickly drop what you're doing to get him to the potty, then keep the diaper on. Or you may want to put plastic panties over the training pants.

As you start to use training pants, begin to tell your child there are "correct" and "incorrect" places to pee. By now, your child will clearly understand all the language associated with this process. When you find a wet panty, take it off and replace it with a diaper. As you do so, be sure to explain carefully that "you are not supposed to pee in the panty. You are supposed to pee in the potty. You wet this panty, so we have to put a diaper on."

Encourage Independence

When you put the diaper on, do so in a positive, matter-of-fact manner. Don't let it be seen as punishment. Tell your child he must put a diaper on because his underwear got wet, as if it's no big deal to you. This lets your child know that his actions dictate whether he gets to wear a panty or a diaper. It gives your tot a sense of control. Training pants feel "neat," and toddlers like them. If he wets the panty and has to shift back into the diaper each time, he'll come to recognize that if he had gone to the potty, he'd still have the "reward" of wearing his new training pants. This will stimulate his growing sense of independence and will encourage him to take on more and more responsibility for his own actions.

Babies can get out of panties long before they can get back into them, so you'll sometimes find your baby playing bare-bottomed. You'll often find that the potty has been used without your being aware of it. And sometimes your child will call you to the potty to show you that he's done it all by himself. Make a big deal out of this! Really show your child how happy and proud you are for him.

Sometimes a child will dump his potty all by himself. He may even spill some of the contents on the floor. Be careful not to blow your top if this happens. He is trying to mirror your behavior by doing what you do. If you don't feel comfortable with him emptying the potty by himself, tell him you'd still like to help with this chore for a just little while longer. Then do it together. Make it fun.

After your child has used the potty alone several times in a row, stop taking him to it *unless he comes to you* for help first. Let him do it on his own for as long as he can. Expect to have some accidents during the next few weeks. It's not uncommon for a child to call you to show where he made a puddle. If this occurs, explain that it was an accident. Talk about it, but don't lose your cool. Help him into a clean pair of pants and clean up the mess. Then, *do not* refer to the accident again. It's over. Move ahead and don't make it an issue.

When your child consistently lets you know when he needs to get on the potty, and when "accidents" are less frequent, you can start using training pants exclusively, except when your child is sleeping. (You may, however, want to use a plastic panty over the training pants for extra peace of mind.)

If your child begins to have more than a few accidents, then take control of the situation again and go back to the "if you wet your panty, we have to put a diaper on" system for a while. When he begins to assert himself once again, allow him to continue on his own.

Soon your child will finalize his training on his own. You'll still need to help out with wiping and getting pants up, along with occasional reminders. But eventually, you'll be able to toss out those diapers for good. Just remember—always approach the potty training with good cheer, applause, love, and a good dose of respect.

STARTING LATER

If you're starting to potty train a baby of eighteen months, your approach should basically be the same as with a baby of seven or eight months—with one difference. A toddler of this age will have greater bladder control and storage capacity. After your child has had a bottle, wait about forty minutes before going to the potty. Then extend the time between trips to the potty from forty minutes to an hour. Try to avoid

getting there *too early*. The goal is for your child to make a strong asso-
ciation between peeing and his potty. The more often he uses his potty
successfully, the better. Study his schedule carefully and make adjustments right away.

The eighteen month old is more mature. He is advancing rapidly
and will naturally have other interesting things on his mind. Keeping
his focus on the potty will not be as easy as it is with a younger baby. In
the beginning, it's best not to interrupt a toddler who's deep in play.
Wait for a natural pause and then take him to the potty.

After the first few weeks, you can proceed much as you would with
a younger baby. Allow your toddler to take a favorite toy (or anything
else he chooses, except food) to the potty with him. It will give him the
feeling of greater control and will help divert his attention should he
begin to fidget.

At the age of eighteen months, a child is at an in-between stage.
Since some toddlers are a little more mature than others, I suggest you
read Chapters Three and Four before you begin your child's training.
You'll need ideas from both sections. If you have already started training and are now having problems, simply stop all training for two
weeks. Think about the steps you have taken, and how you have handled situations up to this point. See if you can figure out how things
went wrong.

If you have had problems, you're probably quite exasperated. Try to
re-adjust your frame of mind, then begin again. I'm sure you'll discover your errors. *Attitude is everything.*

4

The Two Year Old

Most people assume potty training consists of sitting their child on the potty and waiting until something happens, no matter how long it takes. They believe they should create a toileting schedule for their child and stick to it until he "learns," only to become exasperated and demanding when their child doesn't perform on command, or when accidents occur. This is definitely *not* the way to go about potty training.

A child must be allowed to make decisions about his own bodily functions. It is his right to do so. If you remove the sense of control from your child, you introduce a negative into the proceedings that is contrary to the best interest of you and your child. *Failing to respect a child's rights and individuality is the most common mistake parents make.*

Imagine for a moment how you'd feel if someone marched you onto the potty time and again, and demanded that you pee or poop on command. Imagine what kind of attitude you'd develop toward the potty, your body, and the person involved in your training. Yet, this is what many parents do.

If you scold or express disapproval because your child doesn't pee on command, you instill feelings of failure where failure simply does not exist. There is no failure on the potty. You either have to relieve yourself, or you don't. It's that simple. Once your child understands the process, he'll take full responsibility for his toileting needs without your prompting.

Potty training progresses most quickly when a child is stimulated to want to use the toilet. This can't happen when emotional friction is being created by the parent. Training any child requires patience, respect, and insight. By not showing signs of disapproval, you are letting him know he's in control and that you aren't trying to force your will on something as personal as his own bodily functions. Toddlers have the same innate feelings about all this potty stuff as you do. If nobody dictates, no hang-ups are created.

LITTLE CONTRARIANS

The toddler's emotional needs are quite different from a baby's because his priorities at this point in life involve the establishment of his autonomy. As you begin your two year old's training, always keep in mind his growing need to display independence. The best approach to take is one that works with—not against—the two year old's whims. At this age, the average toddler must almost always be given a reason to cooperate with the parent on any level.

Two year olds are contrarians. Tell the two year old it's time to eat and he'll say "No, not hungry." Tell him to pick up his toys and he'll just look at you. Tell him it's time to go and he'll dawdle. It seems that whenever parents tell the two year old what he must do, that becomes the one thing the child is least likely to *want* to do.

Obviously, this attitude cannot be allowed to flourish while training. Since certain parental approaches seem to trigger the toddler's negative response, it is imperative to keep to the path of least resistance.

Toddlers most often respond negatively when faced with yes/no situations. If you ask a two year old if he wants his shirt on, he'll often say no. But if you ask *which* shirt he wants to wear, the yellow or the blue, his mind shifts into another mode. He's being asked to make a decision. Decision-making allows him to affirm his independence. He enjoys this because it makes him feel powerful.

Since the toddler must constantly prove to himself that he has the right and the power to make choices, the opportunity to choose how or when to do something is important to him. Giving your child choices in potty training enables him to express himself. By giving him a feeling of control, you are providing him with a substantial incentive to continue participating.

As training progresses, you should consistently provide new ways for your toddler to satisfy his need to assert himself and make choices. If you have more than one toilet, ask him which one he wants to use. Ask him, "Would you like to go outside after you pee?" With a little creativity on your part, you can come up with many ways of encouraging your toddler to use the potty, while avoiding the "yes, I will/no, I won't" situation.

A STRESS-FREE BEGINNING

Potty training should always be introduced as a fun activity. It should not he presented solely as a means of keeping the diaper dry or as a way of proving how grown-up your child can be.

Trying to *pressure* a child into wanting to use his potty is the least effective approach a parent can take. Pressure creates internal stress and stirs up a child's feelings of insecurity. As a result, the child is most likely to react by not going along with potty training, and might even throw tantrums. This can be avoided mostly by your taking an easy-going attitude toward training. Getting a child into the mood to sit on a potty is easy if there are no pressures to overcome. It's even easier if using the potty is made to be fun. So why have it any other way?

SELF-MOTIVATION

Some parents wrongly assume that rewarding a child with a new toy or trinket will persuade him to try harder to achieve bladder and bowel control. This just doesn't work. A child must be self-motivated to want to sit on a potty. Bribes teach a child how to manipulate; they do not motivate. *How your toddler is made to feel about himself as he goes about his training, as well as his perceptions of the task itself, provide his greatest source of motivation.*

SPARKING INTEREST

Take advantage of normal, everyday situations that tend to stimulate your two year old's curiosity. An obvious opportunity comes when your child follows you into the bathroom. Young children are intensely curious about bathroom behavior. Tots just can't resist tagging along when a parent goes to the toilet. Until now, the toddler has only been a toilet spectator. Most aren't even allowed in the bathroom by themselves, which piques their curiosity all the more.

Toddlers learn by imitating the actions of others. They watch their parents closely in order to better understand how something is done, then they'll try it themselves. The fact that your child shows interest indicates a willingness to participate. If you are urinating and notice that your child is watching you, ask if he'd like to try peeing in the toilet, too. If he says no, respect his reply. But most likely he'll say "yes" because the urge to participate is so strong. Tell him that sitting on the potty is fun. As long as you're not trying to force him, it will be.

POTTY SHOPPING

Ask your child if he'd like to have his own potty to pee in. Then take him with you to get a potty. Have fun shopping for it. In the store, let your child point to the ones he wants to try. Set them on the floor and let him look them over. Look at different types and models. Let him sit on them. Notice how stable the potty is as your child gets up. Observe the style your child is most attracted to. If he likes a type that might present problems, tell him you think it's nice, but "let's go look at some more in another store." Allow your child to have a choice, but don't let him select a potty you feel is wrong. Make sure the fit is right. When you bring the potty home, place it in the room where your child feels most comfortable.

BODILY CONTROL

By the second year, a toddler can be expected to go two or three hours without wetting. He may even stay dry throughout the night. His bladder no longer empties itself involuntarily. When the two year old wets, he pushes first. This is nature's way of indicating that bladder capacity is greater and the sphincter muscles have matured. It does *not* indicate that a toddler is purposely trying to control his bladder; nor does it imply that training will be easier or shorter in duration. It is important not to confuse what the body does naturally with what appears to be a child's command of his body. Your toddler still has much to learn about his body and controlling its functions. Full control comes only with practice and time.

BEGINNING TO TRAIN A TWO YEAR OLD

Every child is different, but each one develops a consistent daily pattern for wetting. Many wake up dry in the morning and after naps and will wet within a few minutes. Others will stay dry for an hour or more after waking. Watch your child throughout the day to determine his patterns. Begin sitting him on the potty a few times a day at approximately the time you'd expect him to wet. As you work with your child, you'll learn his patterns and be able to help him with great accuracy. This will enable him to more fully associate the process of removing the diaper, then sitting on the potty. Be observant. Watch for clues that indicate it's time to go to the potty.

Don't assume that you will be able to establish a new pattern for your child. This will only bring you frustration. If you can't figure out the best time for your child to go, wait about forty minutes after he has had something to drink, then see if he'll sit on the potty. Sit him there for no more than two or three minutes. As you wait, try to hold his attention by talking to him. You may want to give him some small object to play with. Make this a quiet time of gentle communication between the two of you.

Proper timing to urinate soon becomes linked with the sensations felt when the diaper comes off. After a while, just removing the diaper will often stimulate the urge to pee.

TRAINING AS FUN

Let your toddler know that he can make himself pee when he wants to. Make potty training fun. One way to do this is to joke about making pee-pee bubbles as urine hits the water in the toilet or bathtub. To the two year old, this is magic. He feels that he is making something special happen, which he is. The best bubbles happen when he pushes his hardest.

Use your imagination. You'll be surprised to learn how quickly a creative approach will produce results. If your child enjoys making pee-pee bubbles for only a couple of weeks before losing interest, that's okay. During that time, he will have been making an extra effort toward control. That's the important point.

A toddler should be made to feel as if he is in charge as much as possible. If your child sees that you are happy and having a good time, he is more likely to get into the spirit of it all. Your playful attitude is infectious and easily transferred to him. As a result, the training process tends to go more smoothly.

DON'T RUSH

During these first few weeks it's very important to go slowly. Keep diapers dry. Check your child often and change the diaper as soon as he wets or poops. A child who's allowed to stay in wet or poopy diapers becomes complacent to the feel of them. Keeping your child in dry diapers prevents this.

Talk to your toddler as you change him. Tell him he has wet or poopy diapers. Tell him this as a point of information—never with even a hint of disapproval.

As you do all this, you're acquainting your child with his body. In essence, you are helping to develop his whole attitude toward the potty, toilet training, and his body. You want it to be a totally positive experience. So make it a fun, sharing experience.

Emptying the Potty

Show your toddler how you empty the potty and encourage him to flush the toilet. If flushing seems to bother him, don't push. Do it for him. Expect that your child will naturally want to know where his stuff is going. Be prepared to provide a simple explanation. I used to tell my son that his pee-pee was "going to be with all the other pee-pee." He thought that was okay and would happily say "bye-bye" to it each time the toilet was flushed. Use your imagination, but don't lie. Just make things as interesting as you can.

Avoiding Pressure

Don't allow potty training to become a war of wills. Potty training does not involve the teaching of discipline. *Never pressure your child for results.* If you do, you'll create an attitude problem. Just imagine how you'd feel if someone tried to dictate when and where you'd go next, hovering over you all the while, waiting. Always treat your child with respect. If he doesn't have to pee, then simply accept that. The gentler your attitude is, the better. If you show frustration or impatience, you may set training back months.

As you go about training, always take into consideration how the day is progressing for your child. If he's overly tired or fussy, skip sitting him on the potty at that time. Just change his diaper promptly when he wets. If family or guests are visiting, and the normal routine of the house is disrupted, then relax training for the day if it seems to create any friction. Some children just don't want to do it when other people are around. Don't invalidate him by minimizing his feelings. If he does not feel comfortable, then respect that.

Stepping Up Training

After a week or so, when your child has become accustomed to sitting on the potty, begin placing him on it as soon as he wakes up in the morning and right after nap time. Limit sitting on the potty to four or five times a day.

Because the two year old's state of mind is so set on the idea of staying in charge, it is imperative that you not push. Encourage him, but don't let your good intentions develop into a negative situation. Remember that a toddler will not necessarily need to pee simply because you are placing him on his potty. Whenever your child shows resistance, skip that time to sit.

Within a few months, your toddler will have it all figured out. Sitting on the potty will become an easy, familiar task. He will establish his own schedule and will be telling *you* when he has a wet diaper.

Some children will come to you as soon as they wet so they may be changed immediately. Others might wiggle out of their diaper, taking care of the problem on their own.

For most children at this point, getting to the potty on their own before wetting begins can sometimes be a problem. Don't be surprised if your little one tells you he has to pee as he is doing so.

Help your child onto his potty immediately whenever he exhibits a need during the day. Often, he may get onto the potty and find that nothing happens. Be just as supportive when he doesn't wet as you are when he does. Never discourage a child's efforts to master all this. Always show him that you are there for him. This encourages him to communicate with you all the more.

On to Training Pants

Once your child is regularly letting you know it's time to pee, you should begin to gradually move from diapers to training pants. Moving into training pants from a diaper marks the time when a child shifts into a new mode of thinking and responsibility towards staying dry. To the two year old, it is also a very symbolic statement of their progress as well as their parents' recognition of their growing independence. I recommend cotton training pants because they provide the toddler the strongest and most immediate sensations if they wet them, which they absolutely will do. When your child begins to accidentally wet in a cotton training panty, the warmth of urine soaking into the panty will cause an immediate response. So far, pull-ups do not. When a cotton panty becomes wet, urine will continue down the leg and onto the floor. Toddlers are very quick to respond. Some may get upset at first, because suddenly finding themselves standing in a puddle of urine comes as a great shock. They don't like it and they will, therefore, become more vigilant so it doesn't happen again. Potty training is a process. This stage moves by very quickly, so be cool.

Cotton training panties offer various levels of absorbency. Four- and five-ply are best. Terry cloth panties provide the least absorbency, so avoid using them on your child until he has reduced his number of accidents to a minimum.

Make sure the panties you buy are big enough for your child to easily pull down by himself. You don't want him to become frustrated or panicked because his underwear is wadded up! Pay particular attention to the leg openings. There should be enough elastic for ample stretch. If possible, try a pair on your child to be sure. This is one area where being a "size two" might mean wearing a "size four" panty.

I'm sure by now that everyone is aware of *disposable* training pants. Before you decide to use these instead of cotton training pants, please be aware there are differences. Some disposable panties look like diapers; some do not, but they're padded just like diapers. They are made to hold urine just like diapers. If you wet in a pull-up, there is no incentive to catch yourself or stop. Yes, they feel wet, but there is no inconvenience for the toddler to respond to. The only difference is a toddler can pull them up and down without assistance. They do not necessarily inspire the same emotional or physical response from a toddler. These are fine for nighttime wear or if you happen to be out shopping and you know a bathroom might be minutes away. But, when you are in a place where a potty is close, I would advise using real cotton training pants.

Independent Behavior

Toddlers really do enjoy wearing training pants. They are much more comfortable than diapers or disposables. Everything about them feels quite different. Wearing a panty can be very symbolic, as it seems to prove to the toddler that he is now a "big kid."

It's not unusual for a toddler to begin to react differently to situations once the underwear goes on with regularity. Expect to see a surge of independent behavior. Instead of the toddler allowing you to help him into the car, he might demand the right to get in by himself. Or he may want to wash himself without your assistance. As these situations occur, it's important for you to step back and encourage your child's independent behavior.

Approaching Completion

Once your child has developed enough confidence in himself, he will gradually begin to assume more responsibility for his actions. Your toddler will eventually decide that he does not require your assistance to sit on the potty. Instead, he'll decide to do it on his own. This is a very big step for your toddler to make, and it is important that his efforts are not underrated.

A two year old can get out of panties long before he can get back into them, so expect to find your child playing bare-bottomed. Upon inspection you'll discover that the potty has been used without your knowing it. And sometimes your child will call you to the potty to point out how he's done it all by himself. Make a big deal out of this. Show how excited and proud you are of him.

Toddlers love having the upper hand. They also love surprising their parents. Having the power to control his functions successfully without parental assistance is an all-time high for a toddler. This quickly becomes a powerful incentive, reaffirming his independence. However, there will be some inconsistency in his control and potty use. Your child will still need your loving guidance to remind him that it's potty time.

Once your toddler is consistently letting you know when he needs to get on the potty, and when "accidents" seldom occur, you can start using training pants exclusively (except when your child is sleeping). When your child has used the potty alone several times in a row, stop taking him to his potty unless he comes to you for help or begins to have accidents. If your child begins to have more than a few accidents, then take control of the situation again and go back to helping him to the potty for a while. *Do not go back to diapers.* When he begins to assert himself once again, allow him to continue on his own.

Let him take care of it on his own for as long as he can. Expect an occasional accident, though. It's not uncommon for your child to come get you in order to show you a puddle. When this happens, explain that it was an accident. Talk about it, but remain calm. He knows he's not supposed to pee on the floor. It was an accident.

Help him into a clean pair of pants after you clean up the mess. Then, don't refer to the accident again. Move ahead and don't let it become an issue.

Soon your toddler will complete his training on his own. But you'll still need to help out with wiping and getting pants up, and with occasional reminders.

THE TWO AND A HALF YEAR OLD

Developmentally, the two and a half year old has progressed a great deal and has matured considerably. He can feed himself and do all sorts of things. He's more self-assured than he was just a few months earlier. Physically, the older toddler is capable of full bladder and bowel control. He can also communicate his needs more clearly. In many ways, he has become a very independent little person.

The two and a half year old toddler is certainly becoming aware of the inconveniences of wearing a diaper. Most have reached a point where they are unable to tolerate the feel of a wet one. It may even embarrass them. It's at this point that a child, even without any adult assistance, would begin to potty train himself. Being in diapers is a very delicate issue at this age, and should be treated as such. Be considerate as you begin to potty train a child of this age.

The older toddler's increased intellectual development is definitely an asset to potty training. However, he can hardly be considered mature, so keep in mind that you are still dealing with a very young mind. Never try to shame your child because he is still in diapers. If he's in diapers at this age, it's because you haven't helped him to get out of them. No child should be ridiculed because of that.

To begin training a two and a half year old, follow the guidelines in the two year old training section and adapt the ideas to fit the needs of your child. Keep in mind that there will be subtle differences between the ages. Not only is the two and a half year old more mature, he is physically larger. As a result, your child may or may not need to have a potty of his own to use. If he's big enough to be using an adult toilet, then let him. Or, get a simple potty top for him to use. These are inexpensive and can be found anywhere potties are sold. As you shop, keep in mind the shape and size of the toilet seat on which the potty top will be used. Is the opening round or is it oval shaped? This is an important consideration as you select the potty top. Think about where and how you'll be using it. Will it fit securely on your toilet? Are you going to have to remove the seat so that others can use the same toilet, or do you intend it to stay in place? Be sure to read the instructions before you buy. Some seats may be more problematic than others for you to use. If your child seems the least bit uncomfortable sitting up on a regular toilet, get him a potty. Make sure it is very sturdy as you are dealing with a larger child now.

Don't expect overnight results even though you're dealing with an older child. Like the younger child, he must learn things about his body. The greatest part of his training will be spent practicing the art of control. Depending upon the child, training may take anywhere from one to six months to complete.

5

Bowel Training

A good working relationship with one's bowel is one of the most important factors associated with a long and healthy life. Bowel movements should come freely and easily, and with the body's own natural rhythms. Today, adults everywhere fight a daily battle with constipation and hemorrhoids as a direct result of situations they encountered as children during potty training. Certainly diet has much to do with the situation. But inadequate, stressful bowel training has at least as much to do with it. This is an unfortunate situation and something you can help your child to avoid.

There's often more stress associated with bowel training than with anything else a young child encounters. Because they smell and are messy, bowel movements often irritate the adults in the child's life who have to deal with cleaning them up. Yet the bowel movement is very personal to the child. It is a part of his being. A child may feel that if adults think there's something wrong with his bowel movement then there must be something wrong with him personally. Consider it from his point of view and past experience. Most everything he does is great. When he starts to crawl, it's wonderful. When he starts to walk, it's terrific. When he tries to feed himself and makes a big mess, his parents are often amused and offer encouragement. But when he poops and the atmosphere suddenly changes, things aren't so wonderful anymore.

Anyone who displays frustration, annoyance, or intolerance towards a child's bowel movement sends mixed and confusing signals to the child. If a child has to contend with this, his relationship with and control of this natural function can easily become abnormal. This is quite disruptive to the bowel training process.

The elimination of waste is an entirely normal and healthy process. Babies don't have any negative feelings about bowel movements or bowel training until *you* create them. When a child is given the opportunity to learn about his body and its functions without pressure, potty training progresses more rapidly.

Bowel training should be conducted within an atmosphere of approval and acceptance. The experiences a child has during training will lay the foundation for his personal attitudes, and will be with him all his life. How you react, what you say, the impressions you give—all have a direct influence on how your child will come to feel about himself and his bowel functions.

THE WORKINGS OF THE BOWEL

Throughout the day, wave-like intestinal movements propel waste material through the bowel. The encircling muscles contract to squeeze the waste forward. Sometimes intestinal activity is strongly felt, causing a cramping sensation—especially early in the day. At other times, only a vague sensation occurs. Any bowel activity that is strong enough to be felt is a signal that a movement is possible. Obviously, you become aware of bowel activity when you feel enough cramping in that area. But recognizing the more subtle activity enables a person to have a movement at a time that might otherwise have been missed.

It's not necessary to have strong intestinal contractions in order to produce a bowel movement. Therefore, it's important for a child to be given the opportunity to recognize the more subtle activity prior to his movements. As he grows older, familiarity with his body's inner working will enable him to control his bowel easily, instead of having *it* control *him* by failing to work when he wants it to.

BEGINNING BOWEL TRAINING

Bowel training requires a special sense of communication with your child. It also requires that you not pressure him and that you and the other adults in his life not display an aversion toward his bowel movements and to cleaning him afterwards. As with bladder training, progress comes in stages. It doesn't happen overnight.

This bowel training program is divided into three steps and can begin when your child is approximately fifteen months old. The first two steps involve helping him to recognize bowel sensations and to connect those sensations to bowel movements. These first steps take only a few months to complete and do not involve a child actually sitting on a potty. Once your child has gained an awareness of these processes, he'll be better able to actively participate in bowel training. As he gains independence, he will naturally assume more and more responsibility for his bowel movements. Depending upon the child, he may complete training before his second birthday.

Step One

The first step is helping your child to recognize what his body is doing. No matter what the child's age, you begin training by simply pointing out that he is having a bowel movement as it is occurring. It doesn't matter one bit if he's on his potty at the time or pooping in his diaper. You simply want him to start to recognize sensations. Attempts toward actual control will come later. Making him aware of his body as it is functioning is the important thing right now. If your child is clearly aware that he is producing a bowel movement as it is occurring, then move on to Step 2 at the very beginning of bowel training.

As you begin training, whenever your child passes gas, bring it to his attention. This is simply to focus his attention on another function of his body's workings. However, a whiff of gas or a bowel movement should not be made a negative issue. Hard as it sometimes is, never imply to your child that whatever he has done smells bad or causes you displeasure. No holding the nose or "peeeeyewww." It might make your baby feel that something is wrong with him, causing him to become embarrassed or ashamed. Everything you say or do is part of your baby's educational process. He will pick up on even the slightest things.

Since children do not generally have bowel movements when they're on the go, catching them in the act is usually not difficult. If you watch your child closely you'll notice that he will become quite still prior to and during bowel movements. His breathing will deepen and become rhythmic. After a minute or two, it will be all over. Tell your child what's happening as he is having a movement.

Show him the contents of his diaper afterward. Seeing what his body produces allows a toddler to connect the sensations with the final product. It also makes his movements seem more real, because they are no longer just a feeling to him, but something he can actually *see*. Before this point, the toddler is somewhat disconnected from the process because he hasn't made this basic connection. When showing him his movements, a statement like "Hey, look what you just did" is enough. There's no need to make a big production out of it.

As you observe your child, take notice of when his movements normally occur. The majority will have bowel movements in the morning. After a nighttime of inactivity, the colon is easily stimulated by the morning meal. But if there happens to be a lot of excitement in your home or circumstances require a change in his daily routine, it won't be unusual for him to delay his functions until a quieter time comes along. Children are very much like adults in this respect.

Children have bowel movements at all hours of the day—not just in the morning. Every child has different bowel habits, and the regularity of a young child's often fluctuates. Don't expect to catch him in the act every time—just do what you can and be relaxed about it. He'll soon understand. Once you feel your child is always aware of when he is having a bowel movement, it's time to move on to the next step.

Step Two

The second step involves teaching your child to recognize the sensations of bowel activity prior to having a movement. A child doesn't feel the exact same level of intestinal activity prior to all movements. Intensity varies. When you bring his attention to the inner process, he will become attuned to these variations. This will become an asset in later training. By then he will be more apt to notice preliminary bowel activity in time to take control of the situation.

By this time, you should be quite familiar with your child's habits and his body's actions both before and during his movements. As soon as you notice the preliminaries, ask him if he's about to have a bowel movement. (Use your own terminology for it.) He will soon come to recognize the early sensations associated with the process.

Many parents believe that the prime objective of bowel training is to keep the child from messing in his pants. Of course that's part of it, but keep in mind that a child is not a child forever. If a toddler fails to learn how to recognize his body's signals, he will eventually become an *adult* who can't recognize those signals, and constipation could plague him all his life. If a person hasn't learned to recognize the more subtle range of activity that his body produces, he will miss opportunities to have an easy, convenient bowel movement. Instead, he will tighten his sphincters until the sensation passes. Then, sometime later, the colon will begin the process again. Only this time it won't be ignored and the child will be subjected to the pain of cramps and/or large stools. This can create a vicious cycle in which the child holds back a movement for fear of pain, eventually leading to constipation.

Step Three

The third step involves the toddler's developing the ability to consciously control the bowel. This enables him to delay a movement until he can get to a potty. After you've spent a few months helping your child to focus on how his bowel feels prior to and during a movement, you can start to place him on his potty for bowel movements. Most children will be very comfortable with their potties by this time, since bladder training will have begun much earlier.

Begin by gently introducing the idea of pooping in the potty instead of in the diaper. Watch him closely at the time of day when his movements most often occur. When you observe his preliminary signals, sit him on the potty. Tell him that you'd like him to try to have a movement there. A child of this age will clearly indicate "yes" or "no." If he says yes, smile and remain there quietly with him. If he says no, don't force him to sit on the potty any longer.

If you have problems getting your child to sit on the potty long enough to complete the job, find something interesting for him to do that will hold his attention. Books are good choices. I bought my son some magnetic letters that he could stick on the side of the refrigerator in the kitchen, next to the potty. He'd tell me which word he wanted to spell and I'd tell him what letters to get. It was fun and made sitting on the potty easier for him.

Don't assume that you know best when your child needs to have a bowel movement, and never rush him once he is sitting on the potty. If you try to direct your toddler's bowel movements, he will become confused and frustrated. Expecting him to produce a bowel movement just because you'd like him to is not only unrealistic, it's unreasonable. Until now, your child's movements have been free and natural. There's no reason to expect this to change.

At first, placing your child on his potty for a bowel movement may be confusing to him. Since the potty has been used only for urinating up to this point, your child will have to make some mental adjustments. Altering his habit of soiling in his diaper takes a while. As long as you don't dictate (making him feel like this is a "must do" situation), he should find the idea interesting. He already knows quite a lot about his body and how it works—now he just needs to put it all together.

Panic Over Pooping in the Potty

It isn't uncommon for a toddler to go into a near panic the first few times he uses the potty or, particularly, the toilet for bowel movements. When a child experiences something new and unfamiliar, a certain amount of anxiety can be expected. Having his movements go into a potty feels so different that he may easily become unsure or frightened.

An appropriate activity can help keep a child on the potty until he has completed a bowel movement.

I remember my son having a fit the first few times he sat on the potty. Soon, it was an event!

Don't let your child's reaction cause you to panic. Reassure your child and do whatever you can to shift his attention. Empty the potty immediately. Clean it and flush the toilet. Talk to your child the whole time, explaining what has happened and what you are doing for him. Try not to over-talk the situation.

Don't dismiss or make light of your child's fear. This is a real concern. Let him know that you understand and that things are really okay. To a great degree, your compassionate response will determine how long such a fear may last.

Dealing with Accidents

It's important to encourage a child to respond to his body signals. Trust him. Expect that he will do just fine and, in time, he will. Don't worry if your child has accidents. You should expect them. When they do occur, be sure to avoid the use of negative phrasing. Avoid the "not" words: can't, won't, don't. Stay way from phrases like "Why can't you do this right?" or "You're not trying." Negatives only serve to tear down a child's self-esteem, leaving him with feelings of incompetence. Obviously, this has no place in toilet training.

When you deal with accidents, use only positive reinforcements as you talk to your child. Say things like, "Soon you'll do it in the potty all the time" and "Things like this happen sometimes because you're still learning." Find ways to let your child know that you have confidence in him and his abilities to grow and progress.

Timing

Most toddlers don't have a clear concept of time, so getting to a potty in time will be a problem in the beginning. Often, a toddler will come to you just as his movement is starting. If possible, get him to his potty even if the bowel movement has already begun. He's trying, and it's up to you to encourage his efforts. If you decide not to take him to the potty just because the movement is already in progress, you may give him the message that poor timing is reason enough to quit trying. He will perceive his efforts to alert you as unimportant. This can be an emotional letdown for him.

Whenever a child thinks he needs to move his bowels (even when

Potty training takes time. Be patient and supportive.

you don't think he does), he should be encouraged to try. If he does have a movement, praise him. If he does nothing at all, let him know that's fine, too. He's trying, and that's all that matters. If he wants to sit for a bit, make that his choice.

Being Calm and Supportive

Early on, a toddler tends to overreact to his body's signals. He wants to keep his diapers clean, so he's constantly on the lookout for his next bowel movement. It's not unusual for him to confuse passing gas with a coming movement. To him, gas may feel like the beginning of a bowel movement and he won't be sure he can fully control it. This may cause a near panic as he insists upon getting to the potty immediately. Don't try to second-guess the situation. Put him on the potty immediately. This won't happen for long, but it will happen. As soon as he's had some success getting to the potty in time, he'll develop enough confidence in his capabilities.

Don't increase his frustration by becoming frustrated yourself. He needs your understanding and encouragement.

Keep in mind that once a child is on the potty, it will probably take a few minutes before his bowels move. Be patient. Don't keep referring to what you expect of him. He doesn't have to be reminded again and again of what he's there to do. A parent who repeatedly prods a child, does nothing more than create pressure where none should exist. This causes the child's attention to shift from his body to his emotions. The more the parent pushes, the less attention a child is able to give to the actual process at hand.

I don't know of a single person who could have a bowel movement when someone is pushing them to do so. There's no reason why a child should be expected to react any differently. Be considerate. Be patient. Good training allows a child to progress at his own speed. Learning to respond to one's bowel urges and get to a potty takes time and practice. Some children will acquire this ability within a few months; others will take more time. But all children eventually master the process.

Encouraging Participation

Some toddlers have no problem producing a bowel movement when placed on a potty. Others require some incentive. For example, my son had a real fascination with "wet wipes" and constantly wanted to get into them. I started letting him have one every time he sat down on the potty to poop. He used it to wipe himself, too. Even though his "wipe" was more of a pat, it became a part of his own ritual. You'll have to see what works best with your child.

Allow your toddler to assume control at whatever time he chooses. As long as he is gently encouraged to participate in his own potty training, he will not develop negative attitudes toward it. As he enters into a certain stage of independent thinking, assuming total control over his body will become easy. You can't push your child into taking control before he's ready. Pressuring him will only slow down the process.

Once your child has gotten used to having bowel movements in his potty, he will automatically enter into the final phase of training. He'll begin going to the potty to poop all by himself! When this begins, let him make a go of it on his own. If he begins to have accidents, try helping him onto the potty for a few more weeks. Before you know it, he will be taking responsibility for his own movements *without* your help.

It's not unusual for a child who has been using the potty regularly to suddenly regress and begin messing his diapers once again. This has more to do with his state of mind than with bowel training. Try not to become frustrated and don't make an issue out of this. Instead, be patient. Keep in mind that "This, too, shall pass." Nobody really likes sitting in poop.

The Clean-Up

The young toddler faces two obstacles that prevent him from properly cleaning himself after bowel movements. His arms are too short to reach the anal area, and he lacks the necessary level of dexterity. So until your child is at least two and a half to three years old, you're going to have to do his final wiping for him. Most children will insist on participating in the clean-up. Although your child won't be able to clean himself well, let him try anyway before you finish the job for him.

As you begin to teach your child to use toilet paper, encourage him to wipe first, then go over the area yourself to insure a proper job. Always explain to your child that both of you are cleaning his bottom to get all the poop off! Because the toddler has a problem getting to that area, many will try reaching between their legs and wiping from back to front. Girls, especially, should be discouraged from this practice because of the increased risk of infection. Carefully explain that wiping should always be done from *front to back*.

Once your child is physically capable of reaching the area, he should begin taking greater responsibility for cleaning himself. If your child balks at cleaning himself, explain that everybody has to wipe—even Mommies and Daddies. Encourage him by showing a positive attitude toward his accomplishments. He'll soon forget that he ever objected to the idea! Don't allow a child to manipulate you into continuing to do this job for him. There really *does* come a time when helping your child actually becomes counterproductive.

CONSTIPATION AND DIET

Parents often make the assumption that if their child doesn't have a daily bowel movement, he must be constipated. This is not true. Constipation is determined by the stool's consistency, not frequency. For some children, a bowel movement every two days could be considered normal. The chief causes of constipation are dairy products and foods that are low in roughage (fiber), like potatoes, rice cereal, applesauce, bananas, and processed breads and macaroni, to name a few. The residue of these foods tends to be dry or packed by the time it reaches the rectum.

Babies who consume cow's milk are often constipated. This is because the milk turns into large curds when it comes in contact with stomach acid. The curds quickly become hard and dry, producing a potential constipating agent. Babies who are breast-fed don't have this problem unless their system is sabotaged by junk foods and the lack of a balanced diet. Almost 100 percent of mother's milk is digested by babies. If your child is having a problem with constipation or hard stools, don't give him a laxative without a doctor's specific instructions. Instead, cut down on constipating foods and add bulk and fiber to his diet, along with plenty of liquids. Avoid wheat cereals, as wheat often causes reactions, cramps, gas, or diarrhea. Give him fruits (other than bananas) and fruit juices each day.

Don't expect water to soften the stools. Water does little to counteract constipation because it isn't absorbed into the intestines in the same way fruits and vegetable juices are. Water gets directed more toward the kidneys. When a laxative is needed, use a natural one. Barley and oats produce a mild laxative effect. Prune juice has a strong effect. If you use prune juice, do so in small amounts, otherwise diarrhea can be the result. If constipation continues to be a problem, contact your doctor for further instruction.

ANAL FISSURES

If your child experiences a painful movement, it's possible that a hard stool caused the skin to tear at the anal opening. This is called an *anal fissure* and will naturally cause the next bowel movement to hurt as well. If this has occurred, a little Vaseline will help ease the problem. Dab a little on the area after each movement. Do this for a day or two. Sometimes, tears are the result of rubbing too vigorously with dry toilet paper. This scratches the skin, allowing bacteria to flourish. Inflammation follows. Adding a few drops of water to the toilet paper provides a more efficient clean-up and avoids the abrasive effects of dry paper.

Emotional and physical tension can also cause a child to tighten the sphincter muscles. Babies who fear having a movement often hold them back, resulting in constipation. If your toddler seems to be afraid of a bowel movement, quietly distract him while he's on the potty. Sing a song, look at a picture book, or give him a special toy to play with. He'll still be aware of what he's doing, but won't be focusing his *entire* attention on the process. Point out what he's done after the movement is finished. Show enthusiasm. Be calmly reassuring. In this way, after a few successful movements, you'll have helped him past his fear. And remember—don't put a fearful child on an adult toilet. When his stool splashes into the toilet water, it could make him all the more frightened.

THE BIG NO-NO

As horrible as it may seem, it's quite possible to one day find your own sweet child smearing his bowel movement all over the place and having a wonderful time as he does so. This could make you crazy, but don't let it throw you off balance. Small children have absolutely no objection to the sight, smell, or feel of their own stool. Once they get their hands on it, the urge to smoosh it between fingers and toes or to finger paint with it becomes almost irresistible.

If this happens with your child, above all, try to remain calm. How you react, what you say, and how you say it will be remembered for a long time. Treat the situation calmly, as you would any other. Let your child know that playing in poop is a no-no. As you clean up the mess, firmly explain that poop goes in the diaper or in the potty, *not* in his hair or on the bars of his crib. Keep in mind his immaturity and total innocence. Don't belittle him. Just clean up the mess and keep your fingers crossed that it won't happen again. Most likely, it won't

LONG-TERM EFFECTS OF TEASING

Teasing is a part of life. It's one of the ways we have fun with each other. But we must be very careful when it comes to teasing young children. You may say something in jest that a child will take very seriously. Your comments about smelly diapers, poop, genitals, or anything else associated with elimination or potty training may make your child feel that you are criticizing him. Such teasing can have an adverse effect on your child's self-image.

From the time a child's first diaper is changed, he is subjected to comments about the contents. Parents think nothing of making a big deal out of a smelly diaper in front of their babies. And if anyone else is in the room, there may be jokes, further discussion, and wrinkled noses. Just because a baby doesn't fully understand everything said doesn't mean impressions aren't made. They are. A lot of teasing centers on the subject of passing gas. Adults seldom make comments to other adults when they pass wind. But few adults seem able to resist teasing a child about it. Acting startled, smiling, and asking, "Did you toot?" isn't considered critical teasing. But saying something like, "Oh, wow, who stunk up the room?" and making a big issue out of it can have a lasting negative effect on your child.

Babies absorb these kinds of reactions like a sponge. Unable to reason out a teasing person's motive, they take most things at face value. To a child, comments of a personal nature are truthful statements. He may not get the joke. If a child's response to teasing appears to be one of embarrassment and discomfort, he may believe that a critical judgment has been made about him. He could begin to feel that something might be wrong with him. Many parents fail to understand how teasing can create such an impression because they fail to see the situation in full. Adults have the capacity to reason; babies do not. It's that simple. Children learn to judge themselves through the actions and reactions of others. What they see and hear in their own home carries great weight. If you really can't resist the urge to tease, then *make sure your child understands that you are playing*. And please don't be critical or run the joke into the ground. Don't embarrass or shame your child. If you make a joke that results in a confused look on his face, then stop. Take the time to reassure him that all is well, that you love him, and that you were only playing.

6

Thoughts for All Ages

Every child goes through potty training in his own unique way. So does every parent. Because circumstances vary in each home, there may be situations affecting the training process that will require your special attention. Divorce, illness, or a new baby in the family involve high levels of stress and create distractions for a toddler who is being potty trained. A family member who teases the child or who refuses to participate in the training process can also distract the child and get in the way of his progress. This chapter contains suggestions for the parent who encounters such problems. It also offers some thoughts for the working parent.

AVOIDING NEGATIVITY

Potty training your baby is a family affair, and everyone should be made aware of the dos and don'ts of training. A father's role is especially important. Men often brag about their refusal to change a diaper or to participate in any way in the training. This is ridiculous, and doesn't add to the masculine image at all. *And it's bad for your baby.* A baby develops his sense of importance and self-esteem through his parents' eyes. Their attitudes tell him that he's loved, accepted, and has a place in the world. A child is naturally going to become suspicious upon hearing Dad proclaim that diapering or potty training is something he's not going to do.

Babies understand things intuitively. Don't underestimate their little minds just because they aren't talking. If Dad (or anyone else) complains or shows displeasure about the baby's natural functions, your child will quickly get the idea that something about his body is bad. This immediately creates a very negative self-impression in a child. Not only does this

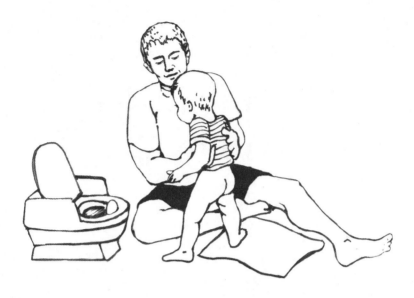

Both Mom and Dad should be involved in the toilet-training process.

make training more difficult, it can give your child a psychological scar he'll carry with him for the rest of his life. This is such an unfortunate problem. If this is an issue in your home, try to overcome it for the sake of your child. Tell anyone who acts in this way to grow up!

A SPECIAL CONSIDERATION

At about the same time toddlers are being potty trained, they are also rediscovering their genitals. This is normal and important behavior. A child must become completely familiar with all his body parts. If a parent starts slapping hands, or telling the child that touching there is wrong, the toddler will make negative connections between his genitals, himself, and potty training. He may come to believe he's "dirty" in some way. This can drastically lower a child's self-esteem.

A toddler simply doesn't comprehend any so-called differences between his ears, nose, toes, or genitals. They are all *him*. It makes no sense to a child why he can play with his toes but not with his genitals. Because boys routinely touch their penis when urinating, they fail to see any logic in why they aren't supposed to touch it at any other time. Don't misdirect a child's focus by bringing such a negative element to his attention. Your child's need to constantly touch himself will pass. But impressions you give him about his genitals will not.

UNEXPECTED OCCURRENCES

If you and your child are experiencing a difficult family situation, such as a death or divorce, or if you're having to adjust to a new environment as the result of a move, it would be best to delay or ease up on training until the child feels more secure. High levels of stress are not conducive to a successful training experience. When a child has to deal with an overly-anxious adult, he becomes anxious himself. This type of anxiety produces insecurity with all the trappings. Under such circumstances, there's no need to further burden a child with a consistent training program. Ease up. If training has already begun, sitting your child on the potty when he wakes up in the morning and after naps would be quite acceptable as a temporary arrangement. If this appears to be too much for your child to handle, then stop training for a while.

Keep in mind that it's not uncommon for a child to regress somewhat when living in a highly stressful situation. So don't worry if he seems to be losing the control he has already achieved. It will return. Your child will indicate when he's ready to deal with sitting on a potty again. Be patient. Training is more than achieving control. It's a very personal experience that requires a pleasant atmosphere. If this means waiting for stress to subside, then wait.

TRAINING PANTS: REGULAR OR DISPOSABLE?

There are disposable training pants that are advertised as being "just like the real thing." But that's not so. There are differences between regular and disposable types. To be fair, I think these differences should be discussed. For those of you who have never witnessed a toddler who has just graduated into training pants, the response to the single act of putting on those made of cotton for the first time is very consistent. They look at and admire the new panty. They invariably stroke and pat them. Moving into training pants from a diaper marks a time when a child shifts into a new mode of thinking and responsibility toward staying dry. It represents to a child a shift in the way their parents regard them. All of this is very positive reinforcement for a toddler. They know they've progressed, and the training pant symbolizes of this change.

The feel of a cotton panty, as compared to the diaper, is a constant reminder. The cotton training pant feels different in every way, even for children who have been wearing cotton diapers. Cotton training pants are soft and smooth fitting. They don't crinkle, and they look different. There is no bulk anywhere. They don't come out of a box. If your child accidentally begins to wet in them, the warmth of urine soaking into the panty causes an immediate response. Unlike the disposable, when you wet the cotton panty, urine will run down the leg and usually onto the floor. This difference in clothing is important because it signifies change in a very physical way to your child.

All of the disposable pants that I have seen look exactly like a disposable diaper. Even though they are designed for a toddler to be able to pull up and down, they still *look* and *feel* like a diaper. Although some are cotton on the outside, they convey your lack of confidence in your child's capability to stay dry. A child quickly discovers that if they wet in one of these, no one is going to know. There are no leaks and no real inconveniences. And the sensory reminder it gives the child of feeling wet, when, in fact, he is, is greatly diminished. This is a big disadvantage in the potty training process. The only advantage to disposable pants is that they don't have to be washed—which is no advantage to your child whatsoever.

Please keep in mind the changes that a *regular* cotton training pant presents to your child. Small children respond quickly to sensory changes. Cotton training pants not only look different; most importantly they *are* different. This difference is significant and can elicit a positive response from a toddler who is nearing the end of potty training. Many parents notice as soon as the cotton underwear goes on, their children seem to acquire a new level of confidence in their capability to stay dry. As any parent who has ever butted heads with his offspring toward the end of potty training can testify, attitude has a lot do with when a child takes on full responsibility for toileting. Potty training should proceed in a consistent and positive manner. The panty represents a most positive last step in training.

WITHOUT A POTTY

During the course of training, you should let your child go to the bathroom somewhere other than on the potty. This experience should be offered *before* your child's toileting ideas become set. It has been every parent's experience that as soon as you're about as far from a bathroom as you can get, your child will have to go. Many parents let their children use the great outdoors in the summertime. Sometimes you might even suggest your child pee in a cup or pail. It may sound silly to encourage this, but there will come a time when there won't be a restroom available. Or your child may be asked for a urine specimen at the doctor's office. It could cause some unnecessary stress if the child thinks of the toilet as the *only* place to go. Many adults find it impossible to relieve themselves anywhere other than in the toilet, no matter how hard they try. This is the direct result of fixations that they developed in childhood.

This is one area I forgot to consider in my daughter's training. As a result, it caused her problems. The first time I realized this, we were driving through Arkansas during a heavy thunderstorm. It was about midnight, and we were in the middle of nowhere when Tiffany announced that she had to pee. She was twenty-five months old and had been completely potty trained for quite some time, so there was no way she was going to wet her pants. At first I told her she was going to have to wait because there was no restroom around. Within minutes she began fussing and telling us that she had to go right then and there.

Since we had nowhere to stop in the heavy downpour, I found a cup for her to use. I will never forget the look of horror on her face when I presented her with that cup to pee in. She thought that I had completely lost my mind. After all, you *drink* from cups, and as far as she was concerned that was *all* you did with them. She sat back down and stared at me in utter disbelief as her father and I tried to convince her it was all right to use a cup in an emergency like this. We told her stories about how we had done precisely the same thing and that it was okay to do so. But she was adamant in her refusal to participate in something as offensive as that. The poor child held it in for another hour before relief finally came. With all of that rain, it must have been the longest hour she ever spent.

THE BENEFITS OF SUMMER

Summer is especially wonderful when you're a toddler. After being indoors for most of the winter, going out and getting dirty can be a fine time indeed. Once outside, most toddlers don't want to go back into the house for any reason—not even to sit on the potty. So, many parents allow their babies to pee outside. Kids like to pee outdoors. It's great fun and a much enjoyed change of pace. Since it is so much fun, toddlers tend to pay close attention to what they're doing as they do it. This focused awareness is excellent practice and has its own special reward for the child.

Not only do children like to pee outside, *they also like to go outside just to do it.* If your child is playing inside and tells you he needs to pee, take advantage of the situation. Ask him if he wants to pee outside. Most children will be delighted with the opportunity. It doesn't take long for a child to realize that by wetting his diaper he misses the chance to pee in the grass or to watch it fall on the sand or ground. Once the idea sticks, most toddlers somehow manage to control their bladders more efficiently in order to get the privilege of going outside.

Some children enjoy peeing on the ground so much that as soon as they dribble a few drops, they may run to another spot and try to do some more. Boys, especially, find this a fun thing to do, and it gives even the shortest toddler the freedom to stand and pee just like the big guys do. Outings such as this give a child more practice and often become a nice incentive to keep dry. Before long, what started out as a fun thing provides a very interesting way to complete bladder training. Even if you find that there are no opportunities for your child to go outdoors, you can still tell him about being able to do so when necessary. This way, you will at least be introducing the concept to your child.

TOTS AND THEIR POTS

If allowed, toddlers will often incorporate their potties into their play activities. Putting their favorite toy on the potty can be great fun. Strange as it may seem to a parent, some will even place cars and trucks on the potty, too.

Kids hold their favorite toys in high regard and will naturally want to share the potty chair with them. They also like to imitate what they've seen you do. They might decide to put on your shoes or take a book or magazine with them as they head to the potty. Or perhaps they'll take something to drink and their play phone instead. I recommend that you don't discourage this. Acting out in imaginative ways helps children integrate what they are learning. It also puts them in the drivers' seat. As long as no food is put into the potty, anything else should be fair game. Keep the potty clean and don't worry about what others may say about toilet etiquette. Keep things in perspective.

Often, toddlers like to put their favorite toys on the potty.

SEPARATING OUTDOOR PLAY FROM TOILETING

Many parents take their toddlers outdoors to play, only to find it difficult to get them to go back indoors. Once parents feel it's time for their child to go back indoors, many make the mistake of using the presence of their child's dirty diaper as a reason to go inside. I suppose they feel a definite need to justify going indoors, either to avoid having to deal with a temper tantrum or perhaps because they feel a little bit guilty for ending their child's good time. Whatever the reason, the excuse usually works, so the parent continues the routine. Although I understand this point of view, I really don't approve of using the diaper as an excuse to go in from play.

Toddlers are very trusting of their parents and I believe if they realized at first that going in for a diaper change meant staying in, they wouldn't go in so easily. Once the child is back indoors, that realization could come as a sudden shock of disappointment that, I imagine, must feel quite unfair. For some children, this type of experience can lead to problems later on. Parents tend to forget that a younger child reasons situations much differently than they might expect. Logic often doesn't apply to the one and two year old's thinking. By repeatedly using your child's messy diaper as an excuse to go indoors, you can ingrain into his mind that taking care of one's personal needs means the end of play. Before you know it, a bodily function becomes directly linked to a negative impression. Once this child is perhaps four or five, situations that naturally occur in life can easily recreate that first negative impression.

The older child who is outside having a great time is often unhappy if playtime ends early. This is natural. Most adults remember incidents in their own childhood when they walked into the house to go to the bathroom only to have Mom say: "Time to stay in." The typical reaction was, "If only I'd held it or used someone else's bathroom, I could have played longer." This is when issues can get confused in a child's mind. For some, instead of recognizing that playtime is ending simply because it's time, the ending becomes directly linked to toileting. The child's confusion leads to a scenario of avoiding his parents by wetting his pants during outdoor play. Once he wets his pants a time or two and the giggles subside, he seems to easily ignore the fact that he's wet: It seems that for some, the need to play is great enough that the idea of wet pants is less an issue than having to miss out on playing outside.

Most parents have a really hard time psychologically dealing with this type of situation. Many feel their reputation as a competent parent is clearly on the line. They know their children are capable of keeping dry, so they see the situation as nothing short of rebellious. Punishment doesn't help. So what's a parent to do? Obviously, you must separate the issues of toileting from playtime. I think this type of scenario can be corrected once a parent sees what the real issue is. The child simply needs reassurance that going to the bathroom won't necessarily mean the end of play. You can do this a number of ways. Perhaps one hour or more before you would ordinarily have your child stop playing and come inside, get him to come in and go to the bathroom, then send him back out to play. Reprogram the situation. You might tell him if he wets his pants, then playtime is over, period, regardless of what time it is. Once the realization hits that it takes only a minute to go to the bathroom and then it's back to play, the situation will be resolved. Toileting will no longer be associated as a potential conflict.

Children love trying different positions when using the toilet.

USING THE BIG POTTY

Toddlers are a lot of fun once they begin using the big toilet. They insist on trying out every possible position: facing the back of the toilet, squatting, sitting sideways. Some will even stand on the rim of the toilet. Boys are obviously the best equipped to pull this one off. Kids love trying new positions. And there's no reason to discourage this. As long as what's coming out goes into the right spot, why make a fuss?

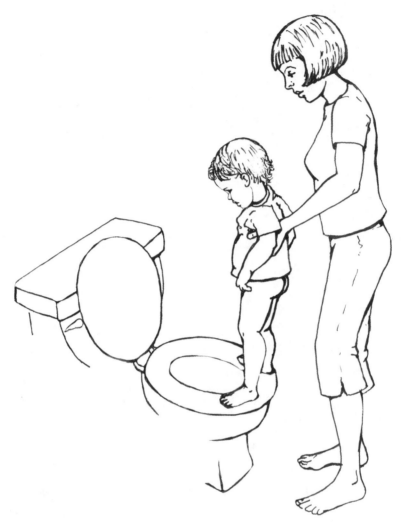

Standing on the rim of the toilet seat.

STANDING UP

Boys generally begin bladder training sitting down. After a while, their desire to imitate Dad or other boys motivates them to stand. It's not unusual for a toddler as young as sixteen months to want to stand up to pee. At this age, he might suddenly stand up on the rim of the toilet seat to go. Or, without thinking of the consequences, he might stand in front of the toilet and pee on the floor.

Standing on the seat works amazingly well for some little boys. But even if your child's aim is off, don't discourage him. Some children have a tendency to overshoot the toilet if they're standing on the seat, so be prepared to get him a stool or platform sturdy enough to safely stand on. Find something that will provide enough height for him to reach over the rim of the toilet. If your child wants to try standing directly on the rim, make sure that you are with him. Be firm. This is a safety issue.

There's really no set time when boys begin standing while peeing. Some try early, some wait a while. If your son shows no interest in it, then don't push. Sooner or later, he will.

HAND WASHING

Many parents go overboard when it comes to washing hands. They insist that their child wash every time they use the potty because they relate it to proper bathroom etiquette. Requiring a child to wash after using the potty is certainly in order if they've gotten something on their hands. But many parents require their child to wash no matter what.

"You wash when you're dirty." That's what children are taught. If they have to wash simply because they've touched themselves, it may tell them that their private parts are dirty in some mysterious way. This is unhealthy, and it leads to a negative self-image.

When your child gets off the potty, ask, "Did you get any pee or poop on your hands?" If he did, you can bet he'll find it. If something is on his hands, help him wash. Otherwise, don't insist on an unnecessary ritual. However, if you are using a public restroom, do require your child to wash his hands. Explain that colds and other illnesses are passed easily in public restrooms. So, this is where we always want to wash our hands.

NEARING COMPLETION

As a child reaches the final stages of training, his ability to control his sphincter muscles increases. He realizes that he is becoming the master of his bladder and will want to discover just how far his control can go. He'll try to hold back peeing as long as he possibly can. He's testing his limits, and sometimes he'll wait just a little too long. You may see him walking with his knees together or holding his hand between his legs. You'll ask him if he has to pee. He'll say "no." This is a natural situation and you should gently encourage him to stop what he's doing and take time to empty his bladder.

Be playful about it, rather than dictatorial. If you know he needs to go but he says "no," don't acknowledge the no. Act as if you didn't hear it. Quickly try to focus his attention on the potty. Say something like, "I'll bet I can get there before you do." Or if you're outside, you may say something like, "Oh, look at this little pile of sand. Come here and pee on it." Whatever strikes your fancy will probably work fine.

OLDER TODDLERS WHO WON'T GIVE UP THE POTTY

Let's face it. Once a child is potty trained and is clearly big enough to use a toilet, the idea of emptying a potty gets old really fast. But getting an older toddler to give up the potty chair can be a real dilemma, indeed. The fact is, some toddlers love their potties. They prefer them to the toilet and will balk every time their parent so much as suggests they use one. So, there they sit, knees to their chin, absolutely ignoring your displeasure. What's a parent to do?

This is one situation that I can identify with, because I went through this exact scenario with my son. Here is how we handled it. My son was really into building things, so my husband came up with an idea to build a footstool for the bathroom. It consisted of four boards hammered together. We told our son that he and his dad would build it so he would have something to rest his feet on when he started using the big toilet. It would make sitting on the toilet easier and more comfortable. So, the project began. They had to measure how high and wide the footstool had to be. Of course this gave Josh plenty of opportunity to offer his opinions, which suited him just fine. Josh was also allowed to paint it. When it dried, we suggested he try it out right away. He did, but obviously still preferred his potty chair. Every now and then, I'd suggest he give the footstool another go.

After about a week of this, I found an opportunity to move the potty chair out to the garage. We were expecting guests for a visit, so I told Josh I wanted to make more room in the bathroom and implied that he'd be able to use it again after the visitors left. Until then, he could use the toilet with his new footstool. I had also bought some new books for him to read when he was in the bathroom to make things all the more interesting. One week later, our guests had come and gone and Josh had almost forgotten about his potty chair. The few times he brought it up, I'd ask him to please use the toilet because I was too busy to stop what I was doing to get the potty. Within another week or so, he no longer asked for it. During the time of transition from potty chair to toilet, no overt pressure to give up the potty chair ever occurred.

Occasionally, we offered a positive remark about the footstool, but little was said about the toilet. Since the little wooden stool was a source of pride, it became a positive focal point. Still, it took nearly a month for Josh to completely let go of his potty chair. You might choose to handle your situation differently. That's okay. I feel that changes should always be adjusted to fit the child's personality. I have a friend who put a TV tray next to the toilet along with a special coloring book and crayons. The only way her daughter could easily use them was to sit on the toilet, which is what she promptly did. Children are all different. What interests one will not necessarily interest another. So it's up to the parent to find the easiest, most positive way to persuade their youngster to use the toilet.

If you are fighting with your child or if you find them in tears at the thought of leaving their potties behind, then you probably should reassess the situation. Are you moving too fast? Talking about it too much? Most importantly, is your child really ready for the change? Pressuring comes in many ways. Change should come gently. It should not be made to feel threatening.

A LITTLE PRIVACY PLEASE

Sometimes around the age of three years, many children decide they want their privacy when on the toilet. Instead of stating this directly, most declare their independence by simply locking the bathroom door. Although there isn't anything wrong with this, parents tend to overreact once they find themselves locked out. This is not an unnatural first response, since most have spent a good deal of energy keeping their baby out of the bathroom for safety's sake. However, once your child reaches this state of mind, it's time for you to readjust your way of thinking. This is not the type of situation that's going to fade away quickly, so do give some thought to how you are going to handle yourself when this time comes.

If you have a problem with a locked door, then I suggest you at least come to terms with a closed one. Don't demand that your child leave the door open or imply that some sort of mischief might be going on. Instead, make it clear that a closed door is good enough and that you will make sure no one will walk in when the door is shut. Then, make sure no one does! If safety is still an issue in your home, then child-proof all the areas that need to be. Explain to your child any guidelines you might have and let him know that he must abide by them. I always felt a little uncomfortable with the door locked because I worried about something unforeseen happening. I told my children that I wouldn't walk in, but they had to leave the door unlocked just in case they needed to call me for something. They never had an accident, but there were times when the toilet paper ran out and my little one was quite relieved that good ole Mom had access.

A private moment.

How you react to the closed door quickly shows your child how much you respect him and his need for privacy. Walking in on a young child simply because you want to is a sign of disrespect and may quickly make this a major issue in your home. Never assume that children don't need or require privacy, because they do. It's all a part of growing up and setting boundaries. Once this very basic need is satisfied, things will change quickly. Suddenly, the same child who yelled at you to get out of the bathroom will begin inviting guests in—selectively, of course. And for a while you can expect to be at the very bottom of their guest list. But in time, even that will change.

BATHROOM FRIENDS

Experience tells us that most young children enjoy having company when they're sitting on the toilet. Oftentimes, from their point of view, the more company the better. The bathroom is a great place to visit. For some parents this "social" setting is very disturbing, and many really don't know how to handle the idea, particularly when boys and girls in mixed company may be involved. Basically, parents get uncomfortable because they're not sure of what's going on when kids get together in the bathroom. My advice is to keep this in perspective. You are dealing with a child who is full of innocence. Otherwise, you might overreact to the most innocent of gatherings, creating the impression that something very bad has occurred. How confusing for a youngster. Kids see social gatherings in the bathroom all the time. In restaurants, they see groups of friends, particularly women, go to the bathroom together. Most likely they've been in the bathroom with you or perhaps with siblings or other relatives. Regardless of how you feel about this matter, it's a common practice in our society.

I found that the best thing to do is handle each situation as it comes, and as diplomatically as possible. Don't be surprised if you find yourself in a situation that catches you off guard. I can recall one time when my daughter was about four years old and had a large group of friends over to play, boys and girls ranging in age from four to seven. I left the room for a few minutes and suddenly everything went dead silent. I returned to see what was happening and found the room empty and the front door locked. Where'd they go? You guessed it, the bathroom. There were more heads in there than I cared to count, all quietly waiting for my daughter to get off the pot. No doubt many parents would have felt uncomfortable witnessing this sharing of such an intimate moment. Fortunately, I was able to see the humor in it and gently encouraged the entourage out to the kitchen for cookies. And so it goes.

CHILDREN AS INDIVIDUALS

Children are unique. Even as babies, each one sees the world different-ly. Most babies have it in their minds that certain things are done in very certain ways. If a parent veers away from that pattern, the baby will balk. Potty training is no exception. Many young children prefer a sense of privacy before they wet or dirty a diaper. They will go into closets, or hide behind house plants or furniture before relieving them-selves. They avoid eye contact with you at all costs. These children are special. They may delight in running around the house butt-naked, but when it comes time to wet or poop, they expect complete privacy.

Once potty training begins, parents are quick to discover that their child's expectations of privacy don't change. It's not that the child can't comprehend using the potty, it's just that they will not use it if the par-ent is within sight. What should a parent do? The only thing you can do is create a setting that insures the feeling of privacy. If you want the potty in the bathroom, place it so that an open cabinet door will block your child's view so he can't see you. You, however, should be able to keep an eye on him. Or, create a small partition using whatever is at hand. We had this same problem with our youngest. I must admit that in the beginning, it was somewhat unnerving to have him sitting there seemingly unsupervised, but we soon got over that. Much to my relief, he never tipped that potty once. As he got a little older, he began using the toilet with the same expectations of complete privacy. Training him was easy as long as we didn't dictate. We simply told him to call us as soon as he was finished.

Parents have to understand that every child is unique and each one expresses his needs differently. Differences must be considered when you're potty training. While some children want privacy, others may demand that you be with them. So go with the flow.

BALKING AT THE POTTY

Sometimes a child will suddenly balk at the idea of sitting on the potty and might even go so far as to not want his diaper changed. Not to worry—this is only a passing problem. New stimulation may have caused a temporary shift in attitude. This could be the result of a recent illness. It could be that teething is causing the baby pain and frustration. If a baby is not feeling well, he just might not want to be bothered. Let him rest and do not push him to use the potty. Being off the potty for a few days should not cause him to regress from the progress that he has already made. Always be sensitive to his frustrations and try not to magnify them by forcing the issue. He'll be back to normal before you know it.

A child might also protest against sitting on his potty because he wants to imitate Mom and Dad and go on the big toilet. Give it a try. If you have a potty top that fits on the big toilet, sit him up there. If you don't have one, either hold him on the toilet and support him with your hands or have him sit facing the back of the toilet. If your child likes it, encourage him to use the big toilet whenever he wants. More than likely, your child will use both the potty and the toilet once he realizes that he has a choice in the matter.

CAN'T FEEL THE WET

If you are using super-absorbent disposable diapers, there is something you must consider. In the beginning of potty training, it's important for a child to learn the feeling of "wet." If the diaper prevents that sensation, then you are going to have a problem. A baby must recognize the difference between wet and dry. The primary reason for changing a dirty diaper immediately is to allow these comparisons to be made. You want your child to recognize that he is wet as soon as he possibly can. For this reason alone, these super-absorbent diapers are not recommended.

THE RUNAWAY CHILD

At some point, all babies will run from their parents when told it's time for a diaper change or time to sit on the potty. Many experts believe that this indicates the child isn't ready for training. They even go so far as to say that the child prefers a dirty diaper and is possessive about its contents. But this line of reasoning is short-sighted. A baby who runs away or refuses to be placed on the potty is simply expressing a sense of independence. This is perfectly normal behavior and shouldn't be treated as anything else. It's not "wrong," and it's not rebellious. This type of behavior occurs in various forms throughout a child's life, but for some reason is often singled out as some kind of warning signal when associated with potty training.

Children between the ages of one and two are just beginning to gain some independence. They'll run just as quickly when their parent says it's time for a bath or a nap. So recognize the situation for what it is. Keep your wits about you and never stifle a child who's trying to assert himself in this manner. This simply means that your baby is shifting into a new phase of development.

Instead of fighting with your child about his running away, give him a little more responsibility in the routine. Perhaps you can have him go get a clean diaper when a change is needed. Or you might let him dispose of the wet one after the change. Allow him to have more participation and stimulate his sense of accomplishment.

THE BLADDER REVOLT

One of the more common situations that occurs with a child during training is wetting his pants while pitching a fit. When this happens to a child who's nearly trained, it is easy for a parent to conclude that he is wetting his pants on purpose. Often, the situation is made worse by scolding or spanking as punishment for this "revolt." You must always remember that your child is still learning to control his body. This type of wetting is involuntary. When a child throws a temper tantrum, he releases a tremendous amount of energy. In effect, his little system overloads and he can lose control of his bladder. If you react to the wetting with anger, you will only make the situation worse. Not only will your child experience an emotional upset, he will be punished for something he was not able to control. This creates tremendous feelings of failure and shame. As a result, accidents will become more frequent because the child's subconscious is retaining those feelings of inadequacy.

If your child wets his pants when he's upset, don't make an issue out of it. Handle the situation as calmly as you can and help him into dry panties. Let this be as natural as wiping away his tears and runny nose. As your child gains emotional maturity, this type of accident will cease to occur.

STRESS AND LOSS OF CONTROL

On occasion, highly stressful situations can cause a child who has developed full bladder and/or bowel control to suddenly lose it. This could be the result of a separation from a parent, the birth of another sibling, a major illness, or a change of houses. This is normal and can even be expected. Some children lose partial control while others lose total control. Usually, this is only a temporary problem that the child will overcome within a few months. But if your child shows no improvement after several months (especially if a total lack of control has occurred), I recommend that you seek help from your pediatrician or a child psychologist.

THE THREE YEAR OLD WHO REFUSES TO BE TRAINED

If your child is three years old and still refusing to be potty trained, I suggest a prompt consultation with your pediatrician. Most often, the refusal to participate at this age indicates an overload of stress in a child's life. Clinging to the diaper, however distasteful it may seem, can be emotionally comforting to the child who doesn't feel quite ready to leave babyhood behind.

Getting out of diapers is very symbolic for a young children. It means they're growing up, they're not babies anymore. Most importantly, they are less dependent on Mom and Dad. All of this is great for the youngster who's feeling emotionally safe and secure within his environment. But for the child who's having difficulty coping with change, the idea of becoming less dependent can be somewhat overwhelming. Unable to deal with anything more, he clings to the diaper.

Obviously, the average three year old is fully capable of being potty trained. As a matter of fact, most three year olds could train themselves—and very quickly. But an overwrought child is a different matter because he is feeling emotionally vulnerable. Children, especially, need constant reassurance in order to work through stressful situations. Sometimes they need more support than we realize. We all recognize that death, divorce, a new baby, or a change of residence is stressful because we feel it too. What parents tend to sometimes overlook is that the cumulative effects of stress in their own lives is also experienced by their children.

For instance, if your child's primary caretaker is experiencing a long-term depression or illness, a child's movement toward independence may be affected. Children are not immune to the pain of others. This is especially true if additional transitions are occurring, such as preschool, or Mom going off to work again. You're going through tough times, but so is your child. The very act of non-participation is actually a coping mechanism. If you react with negativity or respond with anger and criticism for your child's lack of maturity, you'll make matters worse. It's really not unusual for a child of any age to refuse the idea of potty training when he is overly stressed or feeling emotionally vulnerable. But when that child is three years old, parents may sometimes forget this simple fact. Tempers flair and spankings occur. Everyone suffers. If your child is having these types of problems, by all means discuss it with your pediatrician.

BEDWETTING

Sometimes a parent will become concerned if their potty-trained child occasionally wets the bed. In most cases, time will usually take care of the problem. There are a number of contributing factors that can lead to nighttime wetting. For some children, bedwetting is the result of a stressful situation within the home. A new baby, divorce, separation from a parent or friends, a new baby, a move, a new sitter, even the process of beginning preschool or daycare—all are potentially threatening to a child and can create inner conflicts.

Nighttime snacks can also be connected to bedwetting. Be aware that caffeinated drinks, (teas and most soft drinks), milk, and chocolate all act as diuretics. If your child likes to have a drink before bedtime, give him juice or water. Food allergies can also result in a child's wetting the bed. Try making a list of your child's meal plans, snacks, and drinks, particularly what he craves, and see if there is a consistent pattern that can be linked to the wetting of the bed. Often, the causes of wetting can be easily traced and dealt with.

If you have ruled out allergy problems, nighttime snacks, physical issues, and stress, you really can't do more at this time. In the meantime, don't put diapers back on your child, even at night. Diapers infer your lack of confidence in your child's ability to stay dry. To a child, diapers are for babies. This creates inner conflicts that add to the burden of nighttime wetting. Please resist the urge. For greater peace of mind, consider using protective mattress covers. If you want something to protect your bottom sheet as well, you can find unfitted cotton absorbent protective pads that are large enough to cover an entire crib mattress. These can easily be used on a regular bed.

Most children potty train without incident. Approximately 10 percent continue to have bladder control problems. Most of these children have little, if any, problem staying dry during the day, but continue to wet their beds at night. If your child is three years old and still wetting the bed several times a week, it's probably a good idea to have him examined for a possible underlying medical condition.

If there is a family history of bedwetting, be sure to inform your physician for further investigation. A small bladder capacity coupled with the possibility of an irritable bladder are genetic factors that may contribute to a child's tendency to wet the bed. Bladder capacity refers to the amount of urine that can be held before feeling the need to go to the bathroom. An irritable bladder is one in which the contractions are significantly more intense than normal. There are exercises and techniques that can encourage greater bladder capacity and strengthen the sphincter muscles. However, they cannot be forced; your child's maturity level will determine how next to proceed.

Usually a child under four will not be mature enough to begin a program of these exercises. So be prepared to wait and understand that this type of nighttime wetting takes time to correct. Threatening or punishing does not improve the situation and will make the problem worse. It does not help to limit liquids or force your child into the bathroom at all hours. He needs your patience, your assistance, your encouragement, and your love. If your child consistently becomes upset by the wetting, I recommend that he wears pull-ups until the situation improves. However, if he isn't bothered, please don't make him wear the pull-ups.

CYSTITIS

If your child seems to be experiencing any pain while trying to urinate, consult your pediatrician. Cystitis may be the cause. Cystitis is a bladder inflammation that usually causes urinary burning and a frequent and urgent need to urinate. Fever is rarely associated with cystitis. Most physicians believe the infection is likely the result of improper wiping, from the anal area forward. A urinalysis is necessary to determine if your child has this problem. Cystitis is an easily treatable condition that usually responds to medication within forty-eight hours.

PEEING ALL THE TIME

Occasionally the effects of stress will have a somewhat surprising result. Acute stress, anxiety, and sometimes illness can cause sensations that make a child feel the need to relieve himself much more than usual. The bladder may feel full when, in fact, it is not. This can feel quite uncomfortable. In this situation, a child may increase trips to the bathroom from a normal ten or so times a day to twenty or thirty. The amount of urine passed is much less than usual, and there is no burning. Children between four and eight years old are the ones most commonly affected. The most common treatment involves having the child postpone voiding for a minute or so, thereby increasing time intervals between trips until things return to normal.

Most times this problem will resolve itself within a few days. This is a gentle process. A child feels the sensations of a full bladder and naturally wants to relieve himself. If your child is going through this, do not assume it's all in his head and prevent him from going to the bathroom. Doing so will increase anxiety and may well perpetuate the problem. Before making your own diagnosis, please talk with your family doctor. A urinalysis is usually required to verify the diagnosis.

DAYCARE CHILDREN

Potty training is a special concern for parents whose children are in daycare full time. Typical working parents already feel there aren't enough hours in the day. By evening, they still have things to do and the last thing they want added to their list is potty training. They are keenly aware that the primary focus of daycare is to stimulate a child's mental and social development. Yet, few centers are efficiently equipped to deal with potty training.

Even so, there are still things you can do to improve the situation. Take the time to sit and talk to the people who care for your child during the day. With luck, you'll find at least one person who is willing to work with you to contribute a little extra toward potty training. Ask this person to make a special effort to keep your child in dry diapers.

During diaper changes, encourage her to talk to your child, explaining why the diaper is being changed and that she is putting on a dry one. If possible, ask that she put your child on a potty at least once during the morning for approximately two minutes. This should be done at a time when you think your child is likely to urinate.

If the caregiver agrees to work with you on this project, keep tabs on your child's daily success. If he is not urinating in the potty at the time you have scheduled, then readjust the potty time. A few minutes earlier or later may make all the difference. If you are using disposables, this would be a good time to switch to a much less absorbent one. This is important because higher absorbency diapers are meant to draw moisture away from a baby's skin and keep baby dryer. When a child wets the diaper, the opportunity to connect urinating with the sensation of wetness is greatly diminished. This can be a real hindrance to successful potty training.

Understand that most daycare workers do not like the less absorbent diapers because they require more frequent changing and they tend to leak. Be prepared for the possibility that the daycare workers might try to intimidate you into postponing potty training for a while. This is all about them, not your child. If you want to start early, by all means do so.

At home, tend to potty training at every opportunity that comes along. Place your child on the potty as soon as he wakes up if he is dry. Do so again before you leave for work (if he normally wets again at that time). At the end of the day, place your child on the potty again. Keep to a schedule. Pay particular attention to your attitude. Don't rush. Take maximum advantage of weekends and days off to continue training. Read this book again. Adapt it as best you can to your own schedule and that of your child. Cooperation is essential in order for your child to make the step from diapers to underwear. Your attitude is your best assett at this time, so make the most of it.

A FINAL WORD

The key to successful potty training is a stress-free, playful approach. A child learns best when he entertains you as well as himself. He loves games and, most of all, your smiles and enthusiasm. With your help and encouragement, he'll take great pride in sharing this new experience with you. Happy training!

Index

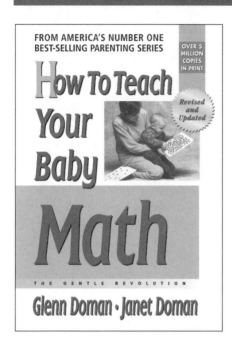

HOW TO TEACH YOUR BABY MATH

Glenn Doman and Janet Doman

Glenn Doman, founder of The Institutes for the Achievement of Human Potential, and his daughter Janet have not only demonstrated that children from birth to age six learn better and faster than older children do, but they have given it practical application.

In *How To Teach Your Baby Math*, they show just how easy and pleasurable it is to teach a young child mathematics through the development of thinking and reasoning skills. In a home program that any parent can follow, the book explains how to begin and expand the math program, how to make and organize necessary materials, and how to more fully develop your child's math potential.

By following this simple daily program in a relaxed and loving way, you will enable your child to experience the joy of learning—as have millions of children the world over.

Glenn Doman, founder of The Institutes for the Achievement of Human Potential in Philadelphia, Pennsylvania, is a pioneer in the field of child brain development. His world-renowned work with brain-injured children led to important discoveries regarding the development of well children. He has lived with, studied, and worked with children in over one hundred nations; he is also best-selling author of the Gentle Revolution Series.

Janet Doman, director of The Institutes and Glenn's daughter, grew up at The Institutes and was actively involved with helping brain-injured by the time she was nine years old. After completing her studies at the University of Pennsylvania, Janet devoted her life to helping parents uncover their children's vast potential.

$13.95 • 256 pages • 6 x 9-inch paperback • ISBN 0-7570-0184-X
$22.95 • 256 pages • 6 x 9-inch hardback • ISBN 0-7570-0189-0

HOW TO TEACH YOUR BABY TO READ

Glenn Doman and Janet Doman

As founder of The Institutes for the Achievement of Human Potential, Glenn Doman has demonstrated time and time again that very young children—from birth to age six—are far more capable of learning than we ever imagined.

In *How To Teach Your Baby To Read*, Doman and his daughter Janet show just how pleasurable and easy it is to teach a young child to read through an at-home program that provides basic skills for academic success. They explain how to begin and expand the reading program, how to make and organize necessary materials, and how to more fully develop your child's reading potential.

By following the simple daily program presented in *How To Teach Your Baby To Read*, you will give your child a powerful advantage that will last a lifetime.

Glenn Doman received his degree in physical therapy from the University of Pennsylvania in 1940, and began pioneering the field of child brain development. In 1955, he founded The Institutes for the Achievement of Human Potential in Philadelphia, Pennsylvania. By the early 1960s, The Institutes' world-renowned work with brain-injured children led to vital discoveries regarding the growth and development of well children. Doman is also the international best-selling author of numerous books, including *How To Teach Your Baby Math, How To Give Your Baby Encyclopedic Knowledge,* and *How To Multiply Your Baby's Intelligence.*

Janet Doman is the director of The Institutes and Glenn's daughter. After completing her studies at the University of Pennsylvania, Janet devoted herself to teaching "the best parents in the world," helping them to discover the vast potential of their babies and their own potential as teachers.

$13.95 • 288 pages • 6 x 9-inch paperback • ISBN 0-7570-0185-8
$22.95 • 288 pages • 6 x 9-inch hardback • ISBN 0-7570-0188-2

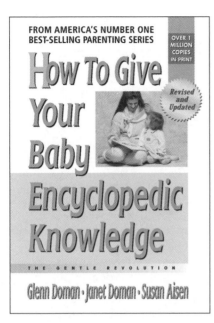

FROM AMERICA'S NUMBER ONE
BEST-SELLING PARENTING SERIES
OVER 1 MILLION COPIES IN PRINT

How To Give Your Baby Encyclopedic Knowledge

Revised and Updated

THE GENTLE REVOLUTION

Glenn Doman · Janet Doman · Susan Aisen

HOW TO GIVE YOUR BABY ENCYCLOPEDIC KNOWLEDGE

Glenn Doman, Janet Doman, and Susan Aisen

How To Give Your Baby Encyclopedic Knowledge shows you just how easy and enjoyable it is to teach a young child about the arts, science, and nature. Through a home program that any parent can follow with ease, your child will be able to recognize the insects in the garden, learn about the countries of the world, discover the beauty of a painting by Vincent Van Gogh, and much, much more.

In a user-friendly style, this book explains how to effectively begin and expand this remarkable program that was developed at The Institutes for the Achievement of Human Potential in Philadelphia, Pennsylvania. It also shows you how to make and organize the program's necessary materials, and how to more fully cultivate your child's learning ability.

Very young children not only can learn, but they can learn far better and faster than older children. Let *How To Give Your Baby Encyclopedic Knowledge* be the first step in your child's lifetime of achievement.

Glenn Doman is a pioneer in the field of child brain development. In 1955, he founded The Institutes for the Achievement of Human Potential in Philadelphia, Pennsylvania. By the early 1960s, The Institutes' world-renowned work with brain-injured children led to vital discoveries regarding the growth and development of well children. Doman is also the international best-selling author of numerous books, including *How To Teach Your Baby Math* and *How To Teach Your Baby To Read.*

Janet Doman is the director of The Institutes and Glenn's daughter. Since childhood, she has worked with her father to help both brain-injured and well children. *Susan Aisen* is the director of The Institutes for the Achievement of Intellectual Excellence. Both Janet and Susan have devoted themselves to teaching "the best parents in the world," helping them to discover the vast potential of their babies and their own potential as teachers.

$13.95 • 318 pages • 6 x 9-inch paperback • ISBN 0-7570-0182-3
$22.95 • 318 pages • 6 x 9-inch hardback • ISBN 0-7570-0190-4

FROM AMERICA'S NUMBER ONE BEST-SELLING PARENTING SERIES

OVER 1 MILLION COPIES IN PRINT

How To Multiply Your Baby's Intelligence

Revised and Updated

THE GENTLE REVOLUTION

Glenn Doman • Janet Doman

HOW TO MULTIPLY YOUR BABY'S INTELLIGENCE

Glenn Doman and Janet Doman

Too often we waste our children's most important years by refusing to allow them to learn everything they can at a time when it is easiest for them to absorb new information. Very young children—from birth to age six—are far more capable of learning than most people realize.

How To Multiply Your Baby's Intelligence provides a remarkable, comprehensive at-home program that was developed at The Institutes for the Achievement of Human Potential in Philadelphia, Pennsylvania. It shows you just how easy and pleasurable it is to teach your young child how to read, to understand mathematics, and to literally multiply his or her overall learning potential. In a user-friendly tone, the book explains how to begin and expand this remarkable proven program. It also shows you how to make and organize necessary materials, and how to more fully develop your child's learning ability.

Let *How To Multiply Your Baby's Intelligence* be your guide. By following its simple daily program in a relaxed and loving way, you will enable your child to experience the joy of learning in preparation for a lifetime of success.

Glenn Doman, founder of The Institutes for the Achievement of Human Potential in Philadelphia, Pennsylvania, is a pioneer in the field of child brain development. His world-renowned work with brain-injured children led to vital discoveries regarding the development of well children. He has lived with, studied, and worked with children in over one hundred nations; he is also best-selling author of the Gentle Revolution Series.

Janet Doman, director of The Institutes and Glenn's daughter, grew up at The Institutes and was actively involved with helping brain-injured by the time she was nine years old. After completing her studies at the University of Pennsylvania, Janet devoted her life to helping parents uncover their children's vast potential.

$15.95 • 400 pages • 6 x 9-inch paperback • ISBN 0-7570-0183-1
$24.95 • 400 pages • 6 x 9-inch hardback • ISBN 0-7570-0191-2

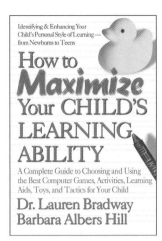

HOW TO MAXIMIZE YOUR CHILD'S LEARNING ABILITY

Identifying & Enhancing Your Child's Personal Style of Learning— from Newborns to Teens

Dr. Lauren Bradway
Barbara Albers Hill

Here is a revolutionary book that offers hundreds of practical ways to influence, encourage, and—most of all—maximize your child's learning ability. Whether your child is a preschooler or a high school teenager, he or she can master almost any skill. This book will show you how.

Over twenty-five years ago, Dr. Lauren Bradway discovered that all children have specific learning styles—that is, they use one of three ways to grasp and remember information. Some learn best through visual stimulation; others, through sound and language; still others, through touch and movement. In *How to Maximize Your Child's Learning Ability*, Dr. Bradway first shows you how to determine your child's inherent style. She then aids you in carefully selecting the toys, games, software programs, and educational strategies that will reinforce the talents and traits your child was born with, and strengthen those skills that need improvement. The result? A happier, more self-assured child with greatly enhanced learning skills.

How to Maximize Your Child's Learning Ability provides the basic concepts that support Dr. Bradway's techniques, simple tests to help you uncover your child's individual learning style, and itemized lists of materials and tactics that will enable you to supercharge your child's learning skills. Here are all the tools you need to start your child on the road to a happy and successful future.

Lauren Bradway is a speech-language pathologist who holds a doctorate in Human Ecology from the University of Oklahoma Health Sciences Center. In addition to maintaining a successful private practice, Dr. Bradway consults with schools and teacher training programs, and reaches families worldwide through her website, *www.helpingchildrengrow.com*.

Barbara Albers Hill received a BA in Psychology and an MS in Education from Hofstra University. A resource teacher in grades one through six, she also writes about topics of interest to parents, contributing to such magazines as *ParentLife*, *American Baby*, and *College Bound*. Ms. Hill is also the author of *Baby Tactics* and the coauthor of *Coping With Mild Traumatic Brain Injury*.

$14.95 • 288 pages • 6 x 9-inch paperback • ISBN 0-7570-0096-7

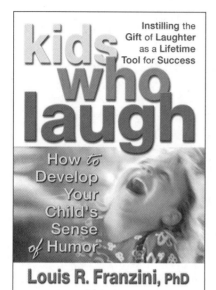

Instilling the Gift of Laughter as a Lifetime Tool for Success

KIDS WHO LAUGH

How to Develop Your Child's Sense of Humor

Louis R. Franzini, PhD

While some children are born with an innate sense of humor, for most kids, a sense of humor is a learned behavior. Unfortunately, most parents never really focus on this important characteristic, and have no idea how to instill it in their children.

Kids Who Laugh is the first book to examine the psychology of humor in children and explore the many benefits humor has to offer, including self-confidence, coping skills, self-control, and so much more. Most important, it offers the actual tools that parents can use to develop a child's healthy and abiding sense of humor. Each activity is fun, easy, and designed to appeal to children of a specific age, ranging from newborns to preteens. Moreover, the author suggests a wide variety of great resources, from amusement parks to movies to magazines, that can further help kids appreciate and create humor.

Whether it's dealing with bullies and teasers or simply making new friends, laughter can make an important difference. With *Kids Who Laugh*, you can give your child a very special present that will last a lifetime—the gift of laughter.

Dr. Louis R. Franzini received his PhD in clinical psychology from the University of Pittsburgh. He is a professor of psychology at San Diego State University in California, where he has taught for over twenty-five years. For over ten years, he has focused his attention on humor research. Dr. Franzini has carefully observed stand-up comedians, has been a stand-up comedian, and has served as president of Laughmasters and Toastmasters International Club. He is the author of two books and numerous articles, and has appeared on radio and television shows throughout North America.

$14.95 • 192 pages • 6 x 9-inch paperback • ISBN 0-7570-0008-8

For more information about our books, visit our website at www.squareonepublishers.com.